Yours Always,
CASABLANCA

A MEMOIR

ROBERT LANGWAY

ISBN 979-8-9988473-0-1 (Paperback)
ISBN 979-8-9988473-1-8 (eBook)

First edition

With much gratitude to ghostwriter, Kerstin Lieff, who is so talented and was so supportive throughout this project.

Senior Editor: Sabrina Young
www.ka-writing.com

Cover and interior formatting by Becky's Graphic Design®, LLC
www.BeckysGraphicDesign.com

Printed in the United States of America

This book is dedicated to Ursula Luisa, my beloved wife and lifelong companion. Luisa's unceasing optimism taught me to always look for that light at the end of the tunnel. Helen Keller once said, "The human being is born with an incurable capacity for making the best of things." This is what Luisa taught me.

Contents

1

Could this be Kismet?

🌿 BOB

"Papa," he said with wide eyes and the intention of a precocious five-year-old. "Tell me a story."

I thought long and hard on this question, and formulated my answer in pieces. I needed to get it right. "Come then. Sit in my lap. I do have a story, and a most important one. It begins and ends in a land far, far away. My tale will take you to Poland and Lithuania, the eastern provinces of Canada, the deserts of Arizona and the beer halls of Germany. We'll step into an era of fur trading and trinket-selling. We'll experience the worst of the war years and the tenderness of love. But you must listen carefully, grandson, as it is your story, too."

MOROCCO, 1954

Morocco is where my story begins and ends. It is a land of paradoxes. Steep, rugged snow-capped mountains and dry, barren deserts. Indigenous Berbers, the Gnaoua, Arabs, Portuguese, and French have inhabited this land since the time of the Phoenicians. The oldest library in the world still exists in Morocco and yet 80 percent of its inhabitants were illiterate until only a few decades ago. You'll as easily see a fat Mercedes zipping by as you'll see donkeys pulling carts heavily laden with wares. Slavery, until

1920, was legal, and Sultans had wealth beyond imagination. Too, Morocco was the first country to recognize the United States before there even was a United States. Called the Treaty of Peace and Friendship, signed by Thomas Jefferson and Sultan Mohammed III, it remains, to this day, the longest-standing peace treaty in American history. Whether city or hamlet, it is a land as much a part of the 21st century as it is still comfortably nestled in the century before. Or, really, any century before that for a thousand years and even more. As the Moroccan proverb most fittingly says: "Everything is possible in Morocco; nothing is certain."

In 1954, the world was fully embroiled in the Cold War. Aside from the fallout shelters you could find in every school and church in America, with the USSR nothing but a large gray splat on our world maps as though it didn't really exist, our military—the strongest in the world—was cautiously prepared for all possibilities. Stretching north to south, from Greenland to Africa, we had constructed bases with warning systems and tactical control radar, bombers and fighter jets, all pointing at our one collective enemy: Moscow.

Because of its pleasant climate and nearly year-round clear skies, Morocco, which lies on the northwest coast of West Africa, was ideal for flight training. There, we had three bases: Nouasseur, Sidi Slimane, and Ben Guerir, Nouasseur being the best equipped with the latest technology. And this is where I landed. Nouasseur. An Airforce man and an air traffic controller.

It was an exciting time; we all felt we were doing something right to defend democracy and freedom. The feeling in the air was that we had a mission to keep the peace, a real and important mission.

In the military we loved acronyms. So, to us, Lou, our commanding officer was always only the "CO." He was a handsome man, goateed, with wavy hair for which he often pulled out a palm-sized comb to keep it nicely slicked back, a pack of Lucky Strikes rolled up in his T-shirt sleeve. You could say he was a greaser, but in a military sense of the word. Clean cut, a sharp dresser, and a man with a large personality.

"Anyone up for Oktoberfest?" he shouted through the air one day as he strode into the mess hall, jingling a few loose coins in his pants' pocket. "I've had a hankering to visit the Eagle's Nest, see what that fool thought of himself back when he held himself to be so Mr. Mighty, and Berchtesgaden is only a short jaunt from Munich. Thinking to rent a rag-top when I get there, maybe even a Mercedes. Anyone up for it?"

Not one of us said no. Who could turn down a free flight and four days in beautiful Bavaria, a place I, for one, had never seen before? Four days of drinking beer and kibitzing with a bunch of my best buddies?

Since it was a military plane that Lou piloted, we all flew as representatives of our country, which meant we dressed in uniform: blue-gray, well-fitted, with four coin-sized silver buttons down the front. Some of us even had pinned-on "chest candy." When we arrived in Munich, we were not hard to identify, and that's no joke. Loud, twangy accents that screamed "American," and yet everyone we met was only too happy to welcome us. The German people were still recovering from the recent war, and seeing US military presence must have given them some sense of security.

What I remember of Oktoberfest was, first, the um-pah-pah-pah of the brass horns, and that the beer could only be brewed in Munich, and then with only three ingredients: barley, water and hops. I remember, too, the party couldn't start until the mayor himself had his first draft, and only after he exclaimed, "*O, zapft is!*" Meaning it has been poured!

Which meant, the party began. With the music playing, men in lederhosen and felt hats with tall feathers coming off the top began dancing the *Schuhplattler* in a circle, slapping their knees and the soles of their shoes. No end to the steins of beer, a liter each, that were being passed around, either.

That's where my memory stops. With the exception of the Hofbräuhaus, of course. It seems as if we lived there after that. It's an old tavern, built originally to supply beer to the Bavarian royalty in the 1500s. They say the Hofbräuhaus alone saved Bavaria during the Thirty Years' War. Instead of fighting, this famous brewery provided their enemy, the Swedes, with over 23,000 liters of beer. Who'd want to, or be able to, fight a war after all that?

Inside, the low-ceilinged room was divided by broad arched columns, delightfully painted with coats of arms and other local motifs. We sat at long picnic-style tables that were entirely covered in carvings from drinkers past—initials of true loves with hearts scratched into the wood, many of which dated from long before the time you or I were even alive. The lighting was perpetually in a state of dimness in contrast to the atmosphere which was full of laughter, sarcasm and the occasional whistling and gesturing at the attractive dirndled waitresses who carried four steins in each hand. But what I noticed most was the carefree language of these people, as if their country had some sort of amnesia to the devastation that had taken place here less than a decade ago.

But back to my story. Where was I? I want to tell you about where I lived, what I did, how my days went. And a very important incident that happened one day, right here, in old Morocco.

On the base of Nouasseur, our living quarters were called "huts." Twenty-five feet square, set in rows with narrow paths between, four enlistees lived together in a hut, four bunks, one in each corner. A potbelly stove sat square in the middle on the wooden floor, and next to it, a metal box with briquettes of black coke to fire up during the chilly months of winter. Each of us, next to our bunk, had our own closet of sorts, really just a locker, in which we could hang our uniforms and civilian clothes as well as keep our boots and personal items tidy. Outside, about thirty feet away, was where our shower rooms and latrines were. On any given morning, you could catch twenty guys there, soaping up in unison, singing in unison, some even whistling, but all of us getting ready for the work ahead.

It was a Thursday afternoon, a dreary November, nothing to write home about. I had just finished my shift at the control tower. My duties had been minimal, as convoys of clouds had been stretching from horizon to horizon all day, not ideal for fighter pilot training. What they needed, and wanted, was clear skies in which they could practice their siting and shooting.

I wasn't ready to return to my hut yet; it was too early for that. So, I decided to check out the United Service Organizations (USO) to see what I could find. The USO was housed in a Quonset hut—a half-circle building made of corrugated steel, which gave the interior nearly 1,000 square feet of usable space that was quite practical for the military: cheap, easy to assemble and quick to tear down when it was time.

The USO made every effort to keep us guys entertained. Even Marilyn Monroe, and later Bob Hope, made the USO part of their tours, but for us at Nouasseur, it was the local artists from nearby Casablanca who came to perform.

I entered from the side entrance which opened into a sort of lounge area. Well-worn easy chairs, a few lamps and stacks of library books were scattered around. I wasn't sure what I was looking for. There was the possibility of a movie. But I had already seen *The High and the Mighty*. It starred John Wayne, and it was good, I liked it, but I wasn't really in the mood.

Music was my next best choice. I rifled through some LPs I'd found sitting against a corner and picked my favorites. Louis Armstrong, Doris Day, Frank Sinatra. . . maybe something else, slow and schmaltzy, then I made my way to a private cubicle to listen. Two other airmen were standing around, busy with something else. But something just wasn't right. I felt antsy and instead of my music, my mind wandered off to the dance tunes coming from elsewhere. My buddy who had told me about the individual listening spaces evidently failed to mention the weekly USO dances. Then, from a voice over a loudspeaker, I heard: "Airmen and ladies, take your seats! Have a look! Masoud, the magical, mystical hypnotist is about to perform. Yes, HE can make YOU do anything!"

I thought to myself, "Sounds more fun than sitting alone in a sound-proof box!" I quickly put away my few records—I couldn't concentrate anyway—and went to see what all the hullabaloo was about.

The room was a little on the dim side. It had a bar, tables, and chairs. Enlisted men and civilian women—most of whom worked on the base—had started gathering around the dance floor, in the center of which was a man busily breaking open a folding chair. He had springy hair and ballooning pants and a fez on his head. Most dramatic were his hands with long brandishing fingers that he waved around his head, inviting volunteers to come forward, volunteers who *swore* they could never be hypnotized.

"Have you ever been hypnotized?" he asked.

"Absolutely never!"

"Well, good then. This will be your first," to which everyone chuckled.

And so it went, one volunteer after another, until a good

handful had stepped forward. Certainly, what he did then was not in the least "hypnotizing." He merely hummed a few lines to what sounded like a Moroccan tune, then whispered something into each one's ear.

Then began the fun. His first candidate was a man we called "Tubbs." Not because we didn't like him. (We actually did.) It was because, out of all of us, he was the one with a few extra pounds around his middle. "Okay, Sweet Pea." the hypnotist said, "You are a very lucky man. You live in a palace. You are a dancer. You belong to Sharrif Saoud's very impressive haram, and tonight, of all the luxurious nights, you, and only you, are to perform for his illustrious guests. As you can see, there are many. Is this not so?"

Tubbs peered around, and in all earnestness, nodded while he took in the crowd. Faintly at first, then progressively louder, over the speakers came the sultry sounds of Moroccan castanets, fiddles and flutes, and without a moment's hesitation, Tubbs began to shake and shimmy around the circle, his belly jiggling to the rhythm, his hands making long V's across his eyes that threw coy looks at his "guests." Oh my, how we couldn't even hold our sides, it was so funny.

And that is when I saw her.

Her face was not unfamiliar; I realized I had seen her before. It had been in the mess hall where we both stood in line for our lunches. I had not thought much about her at the time. After all, I was only in Nouasseur for eighteen months; I was only twenty years old. And I was not interested in starting anything with a woman, especially one who was a foreigner. I'd be back in the States in no time. And then what?

But there she was, again. The girl from the mess hall. She sat cross-legged and wore white pumps. She could have been wearing all white, for all I remember. I can't describe it, really. A navy skirt, knee-length? Perhaps. I can't describe it because it was the picture of her that I remember most: serene and radiant, as if a beam from the ceiling had turned upon her, and her alone.

She was chatting with two other women and didn't really notice me. But I noticed her.

The hypnotist got one last person to make a fool of himself, this time handing him a mop and said, "Do you know your name?"

"Yes, of course I do."

"Do you know it's Mickey Mantle?"

"Yes."

"Say, 'my name is Mickey Mantle.' "

"My name is Mickey Mantle."

"Do you know why you're famous?"

"Yes, of course I do. I'm a switch-hitter! I'm a Hall-of-Famer! I'm the Number One Home-Runner!" The man started swinging the mop, first right-handed, then left-handed, staring off into the dark as if he'd just hit a homer over the fence.

Then, the lights went bright. The DJ grabbed his mic, thanked Massoud, and turned to the crowd. "Don't go away, folks! There's plenty more to come!" After which he busied himself setting up shop on the bandstand where he was about to spin his vinyl. Tubbs never did admit that that was *he* doing all the wiggle-bop on the floor; he denied it until the day he was sent back to the States.

Within minutes, this came over the speakers: "Airmen, pick your partners!"

The DJ placed a 45 on the turntable. It was "Blue Moon." That song will stay with me forever. It was composed by Rogers and Hart, sung by Billy Eckstine, and if I could, I would sing it to you. It's the way Billy croons that gets to me every time. "Blue-oo moo-oon. . . you left me standing alone." That sustained note, "aloooone. . .," the tenor voice melting into the next line, "without a dream in my heart, without a love of my own. . ." Like a beating heart.

I looked over at the pretty woman in white. She saw me, too, this time, and I thought I noticed the corners of her mouth turn up into a slight smile. It was all I needed to go over and ask her to dance. It was too perfect, this moment, this song, and, besides, I thought I had seen her smile.

I rose and began my walk, all the while fearing the worst: She would say no. And then the second worst: My French was really bad. I kept walking. Was the dance floor a mile wide? It felt that way. And now, another fear. My hands. They were wet with nerves.

"Voulez-vous danser avec moi?" I said shyly as I approached her, using the very best, most practiced, French I could summon.

"Mais bien sûr," she responded. She was even more beautiful up close. I noticed her strong eyebrows—which I liked on a woman. It showed character, I'd always thought.

She rose with grace, and together we seemed to glide to the center of the floor. It all felt so enchanted, as if that hypnotist had had everything to do with it.

The next song was Tony Bennett. "Because of You." "There's a song in my heart. . ." I sang the lines inside my head, absorbed in the moment. ". . .forever and never to part. . ."

It was not enough that the words were so right, or that she danced so well, or that her perfume had everything to say about exotic Morocco. It was not enough. That we kept dancing, that was enough.

I attempted, badly, to make conversation, using the little I knew to say in French. "Quel es votre nom?"

"Je m'appelle Ursula," she answered frankly.

A nice German name, I thought, like the waitress in Munich who had been so delightfully rude all afternoon.

"Enchanté," I responded, feeling evermore confident with my foreign language skills. "Je m'appelle Robert." I pronounced "Robert" like "Roe-BARE," trying hard to be the man in the know in this French-ish country. At this, Ursula threw her head back and laughed out loud at my goofy attempt at impressing her.

She took over the conversation from there, much to my relief, as I had run out of things I knew to say in French. She worked for an officer at the base, she said, and yes, she lived in Casablanca, right in the heart of the city. She lived with her mother and two younger siblings. That was her mother, she pointed, sitting next to her friend. And yes, her friend's name was Claudette.

Meanwhile the next record came on. "You Belong to Me." Lyrics I knew by heart, lines that spoke just to me, just to us, just now, in this moment. "Fly the ocean in a silver plane. . . you belong to me. . ." I could not believe Jo Stafford's voice singing exactly what I felt, as if in a dream.

"I love this song!" Ursula blurted. She said it so non-ambiguously, and in a not-even-accented English!

"What?" I said, pulling back to make full contact with her eyes. There was that smile again. "You fooled me!" To which she laughed, again, heartily, and so did I.

We chatted then, on and on. I told her I had seen her before. It was in the mess hall lunch line. She nodded. She'd seen me too. I told her about the food, and how I was now eating stuff I'd never have put in my mouth back in the States, how my Ma sometimes made. . .

"Tell me it was liver!" Ursula cut in.

"It was!" I said, "it was, and now I eat it all the time and. . ." and we both exclaimed, "with fried onions!"

It must have been a popular saying around here or something she heard her boss say, because then, in unison we said, "Eat or starve!" We both laughed, hard. It was like she was breathing at the same time I was, our thoughts moving in tandem.

The three-song set came to an end, and we walked back to her mother and friend. As if the hypnotist had played his magic once again, there was a vacant seat next to hers now, just for me.

Ursula introduced Claudette first. "She doesn't know English," she said. "But we both know how well you know your French, n'est pas?" she teased.

"Oui," I responded. "Enchanté!"

"Enchanté," Claudette replied and clasped her hands into her lap.

To my left sat her mother who quickly wanted to know everything about me. My name, of course (Bob), but also where was I from (Massachusetts), how long was I stationed here (not long) and what were my duties (too many to count). Eleanor was her name, and each time I turned my head back to Ursula, she nodded, as if in agreement.

Claudette, in contrast, said very little and then only in French. Only an occasional "Oui," and otherwise stayed silent. She was a rather plain girl. She wore a plain blouse and slacks. Perhaps she was bashful, not having a clue what we were talking about. I tried my best to include her in conversation, but then Eleanor kept my attention, talking about her daughter, which was most interesting. She told me Ursula had lived in Paris, that it was in the 14th arrondissement, that she had gone to school there, that she worked as a bilingual receptionist, that she had only arrived in Casablanca in March. . .

"What a nice coincidence," I said, turning to the woman on my right. "I also arrived in Casablanca in March," as if it were an intimate discovery made between just the two of us.

"I wasn't always in France, though," Ursula explained. "I'm originally from Germany."

"Another nice coincidence," I replied. "I was just in Germany." I couldn't help but picture the many bright-eyed, blonde women in Munich with their eternally kind and mesmerizing smiles only a few months ago. How attractive they were to me then; how attractive Ursula was to me now.

The DJ announced it had been the last song. "You don't have to go home, folks, but you can't stay here!" he joked as a send-off.

I offered to escort the three ladies out, which they accepted graciously. Outside were three waiting buses, very recognizable, deep blue with the flagship logo, "USO," flanked by three red stars on either side.

My new friends boarded the first bus, Ursula taking a seat at a rear window that she quickly rolled down to say goodbye. My heart jumped to my throat as she peered out at me. "Ursula," I said. "May I ask for your telephone number? I'd like to call you," I stammered. "Do you have a number on the base? Can I see you again?"

I felt like a fool, doubling up on myself like that, but she gave me her greathearted smile and said, "I'd like that very much."

She reached into her purse for a scrap of paper and wrote down the four digits of her number at work.

As the bus rolled off and her beautiful head appeared one more moment out the window, I couldn't help but think how very lucky I was. I had met someone so nice, so attractive. And she wanted to see me again.

The next day, I was on the afternoon shift, 1200 to 1700 hours. It was Friday, and a clear day. Besides a cargo plane bringing in more troops and military equipment, fighter jets landed, flying from any number of locations in Europe, where, at this time of year, it was usually too foggy and too gray for good siting. They arrived nearly every fifteen minutes, here to practice aerial maneuvers and target training.

We saw B-47s and B-36s, all of them equipped to carry bombs and missiles, some even nuclear, but the most impressive were the F-86s, the Sabers, that held their bombs in compartments under the wing. Although I'd only ever witnessed it out in the endless Saharan desert, I knew why they were here and what they were about to do: these guys were rearing to shoot. A jet would fly out ahead that would blast a thick contrail behind, much like what you see when planes write advertising in the sky, their exhaust coming together as words. The fighter jet then, would fly in right up behind and shoot rounds and rounds of armor-piercing incendiary, APIs, right at the white floating lines in the air. *Pop-pop-pop-pop-pop.* Extraordinary to witness, the contrails virtually melting before my eyes, and the jet pilot whooshing off when finished, disappearing as a flash in the distance.

As tower operator, it was my job to guide the jet in for a safe landing. I'd radio for a jeep that carried a large sign on its roof saying, "FOLLOW ME," and slowly he would lead the jet to its resting place where it sat until takeoff once more.

It was a busy afternoon and yet, again and again, my mind slid into thinking about her. Her voice. *I'd like that very much.* An incoming jet. *Her laughter.* As much as I loved being busy at work, on this day, I could not wait for a break. How nice the evening was.

The moment finally came when the air traffic slowed enough that I could go to a phone to call, and I wasted no time. My fellow controllers couldn't figure out what was eating me; I'm usually rather easy-going, not too hurried.

I found a phone and dialed her number, trying to picture where on the base her office was, where was she? Was she wearing a dress? Was she talking to her boss? Would she answer?

A woman picked up, and when I asked to speak to Ursula, she said, "I'm sorry, Sir, but she's not at her desk at the moment."

Oh, the disappointment. But I did not let it deter me. "Will you have her call me when she gets in?" I then quickly gave her my extension. And waited. My hands were sweating again. Five minutes went by. The phone rang. I jumped, I answered.

It was her!

She apologized for having missed me. She said she was happy to hear from me. I told her I would be in Casablanca next Saturday. I said it would be my pleasure to see her again. Did she know a place where we could meet?

Ursula sounded happy to know I wanted to see her. She even suggested I come have lunch at her place with her mother and younger sister and brother. Could I come to their apartment on Rue Voltaire? At noon? She said they would look forward to seeing me; I said I would be glad to join them. She said how much she was looking forward to Saturday; I said, please give my thanks to Eleanor. "For the thoughtful invitation," I added quickly. I hoped my ear-to-ear grin could be felt through the wire.

When we hung up, visions from the night before continued to swirl through my head, and all I could think was: *She said yes.*

2

Bobby, You Have Indian Blood in You

My Aunt Eva knew everything. She lived to be a hundred, and when she told me I was Indian, I was five. I knew she meant it like it was real, but this caused me great consternation. Indians were the bad guys, from my understanding, and they were the ones always being killed. I'd rather she'd said, "You have cowboy blood in you." I could live with that. This quandary puzzled me to no end. So, I decided to ask the next person who knew everything: my mother.

GREAT-GRANDPA LEWIS AND PRINCESS MARGARETTE

Fair Trade

1831–1875

My Ma would not tell a lie, I knew this for a fact. And when I asked her, she was all too eager to tell me.

"You never knew your great-grandpapa," Ma began, "but he was a man of presence." I sat up when I heard this. This was an ancestor I needed to know about. "He made a burly impression, with a thick beard, thick shoulders, and an ever-present faded slouch hat on his head. . ."

Her story took a while to tell, maybe weeks. At night before bed, she'd come to the boys' room to sit and talk, just to me. Here's what she said, nearly all of it accurate.

My great-grandpapa was born in 1831 in Quebec to French and Scotch-Irish parents. Quebec was then known as "Lower Canada." Before that, it was called Nouvelle-France, or "New France." After the Seven Years' War, when the British won dominion over the territory, names became anglicized. Not surprisingly, the French, who had been there for generations, were resistant to this intrusion. But the British now owned most of the land, and most of the industry, so this left the French to do what they did best: the fur trade.

"L'angevin means Angel Wine in French," Ma whispered, hoping not to wake the other boys. It was already late that first night. "It was his surname, which became 'Langway' in time. The settlement where he was born is called Trois Rivières. It means 'Three Rivers.' Three weeks after his birth, he was christened Lewis in the Catholic tradition."

Lewis grew to be a resourceful young man, handsome and keen to earn his way in the world. He was adept at fishing, hunting, and trapping, all skills needed in this untamed land. Lewis, too, had a gift for gab. There was not a person who was not his friend, and he often found himself as a guest at new-found tables, which on occasion included tribal campfires.

He spoke French, the language of his home, but soon became proficient in not only English but also in the tongues of those he did business with—the Algonquin and Abenaki tribes, people whom he encountered often, even as a child. Learning to speak with them was an easy task for Lewis. The native languages exchanged many words from one to the next, and the sentence structure was simple. No articles, no tenses, no adjectives. Subject, object, verb (I, moose, saw) made the ideas clear. Words were used sparingly, but usefully, and many were words the English and the French did not even have. Words like caribou, opossum, moose, raccoon.

Before Lewis was born, a particular fashion ruled the European world. It was the top hat that remained in style for nearly a century. Over the decades this popular men's hat grew ever taller (see Abraham Lincoln), then settled back down to the pork pie and eventually morphed into the newsboy caps of the twentieth century. But that does not matter here. What's important is that they were all made from beaver pelts, and these beaver pelts came from Canada.

Beaver skin was naturally waterproof, and it gave these gallant hats an especially luminescent sheen. The top hat fashion lasted so long across all of Europe, and so extensively among all classes (including the French and British militaries), that the beaver population of Canada was decimated.

Then, in 1850, when Lewis was twenty, full of spunk, and established in his trade, the demand for beaver diminished almost overnight. The fashion in Europe had moved on to silk, which was lighter in weight and cheaper to manufacture. The only animal needed was the silkworm, whose abundance seemed endless. The cost and time for beaver hunting, trapping, killing, skinning, transporting, selling, and then hat-making was essentially erased.

But Lewis was not deterred. It only meant new products and new customers. Mink and martens for women's coats, not to mention the hats of the British King's Guard still needed bear skins. With First Nation peoples still hungry to trade, there continued to be plenty of opportunity for Lewis, as long as he kept moving, which he did.

There were no roads then, no borders to speak of either, no checkpoints. Navigation was by rivers and Indian trails. So, one day, Lewis departed Trois Rivières in his birchbark canoe, paddling and portaging ever southward. What he carried with him was what he traded. Needles, blankets, cloth, kettles, metal pots, tea and alcohol. From the Indians, he received traps and furs which he turned around and sold to the French North West Company or the British Hudson's Bay Trading Company. It didn't matter which. Business was business. You could say he was an international traveling salesman.

He made his way as far south as Portland, Maine, the language now officially English. As hard as he tried, Portland was not good to him. Business slim to none, he moved on and finally arrived at Lake Chaubunagungamaug in Massachusetts. The real name, "Chargoggagoggmanchauggagoggchaubunagungamaugg," comes from the Nipmuc. With forty-four letters, it is the longest name of any geographic feature in the United States, maybe even the longest word in Merriam-Webster's dictionary. No wonder we prefer to call it "Webster Lake" instead.

Herux was the name of the chief who lived at that lake, and Lewis established a strong and lasting trade relationship with him. He was heavy-set for an Indian, not exactly fat, but a big man, with big hands meant for big trading.

Herux had a sister whose native name we no longer remember. She was beautiful and smart and Herux's most trusted business partner. She had a keen mind and an intuition for a fair bargain. When Lewis first laid eyes upon her, he was filled with the same feeling he had on the many nights he lay alone on his furs in the dense forests, staring into the fathomless star-filled night. His breath caught short in his throat.

"Margarette," she answered, her black-coffee eyes boring straight into his when he politely asked what her name was. She did not lower her eyes, as he expected. Instead, she stood, her back straight and tall. Strands of sun-sparked hair blew softly across her face. Strong tanned hands rested lightly upon her dress. Believing she was awaiting a response, Lewis stuttered, "So you have a name I can pronounce!" He meant it as a joke, but he said it in English, and her nod let him know, she knew what he said.

Lewis and Herux made numerous business dealings, always negotiated by Margarette, and all the while Lewis's heart fluttered. Then, finally one pleasant day in 1868, he asked: "Herux, Chief. I wish to marry your sister. She is beautiful; she is smart. I will care for her for all the days of my life."

In these hinterlands, where trappers and traders roamed for months on end, it was not uncommon to take a First Nation woman for a wife. It was a practice sanctioned by the Indians, as, for them, it ensured strong and lasting familial business ties. And so, Herux agreed.

"I imagine the ceremony was out in the forest, according to her tradition. 'Marriage à la façons du pays,' a marriage according to the customs of the land, as the saying in Canada went.

"I imagine she wore a kidskin wedding dress." Ma gazed off into the dark of the room. "Surely, it was carefully beaded with azure glass and gold threads, the best from France. Margarette was a princess, after all. I imagine the ceremony included the offering of tobacco and sacred prayers to the fire. But there are no photos, no history. I only imagine."

It was time to sleep. The story would continue, but first I needed confirmation: "So, I have Indian blood in me?"

"Yes, son, you do."

It is a story now that makes me proud. I come from ancestors who understood their destiny, forged their path, and never looked back. I could live with that.

As the fur trade diminished, profits dwindled and opportunities fizzled. Lewis decided, with his new bride, to homestead a farm near Webster Lake. Over the next years, two daughters arrived and several sons, one of whom was Ovid, my grandpa. Ovid was born in 1875, which made Lewis a very old man. He was forty-four by then.

GRANDPA PETER AND GRANDMA NIKKI
There You Will Find Your Way
1880–1926

Peter Mikolosius was a quiet, serious boy who grew up on a farmstead in a small village in eastern Lithuania in the late 1800s. By the time he was born, Lithuania as a country had pretty much disappeared from the map, having been overrun primarily by the Great Russian Empire. After a famine that took 40 percent of the population, after a system of "Russification" that left most of the country in poverty, thousands of Lithuanian peasants made the arduous journey to America. Between 1868 and 1914, nearly 20 percent of the remaining population departed Lithuania, most of them heading to the United States or Canada. Peter was one.

Nikolina Hedwig Nijinsky, or Nikki as she liked to be called, was a headstrong girl, born in Warsaw, Poland in 1880. By Polish standards, her family was fairly well-off. They had a comfortable home and enough to eat. Her father held the prestige of career officer in the Polish army. It was an official job with a steady income, but the army was weak. The ruling Russians did not allow war machinery, such as tanks or even modern munitions, so Poland's army was a puppet army, and so backward that when Hitler invaded in 1939, the Polish troops arrived on horseback. Poland was defeated within nine days.

Both Lithuania and Poland were in a state of serious decline in the 1800s. Both countries lacked effective governments, and their people were, for the most part, poverty-stricken with little to no opportunity to better themselves.

Around the same time, the largest shipping conglomerate in the world was in Hamburg, Germany. HAPAG (Hamburg-Amerikanische Packetfahrt-Actien Gesellschaft) began as a cargo operation, but soon offered passenger excursions to London and New York.

At first, it was only the rich who could afford such luxury, but a Jewish-German merchant, Albert Ballin, came up with the idea of "steerage decks." These were decks installed far below those given to the first and second-class passengers, allowing HAPAG to sell many more seafaring seats for far cheaper fares and, by so doing, targeting those with limited resources. In other words, the poor. To find clients, Ballin hired a sort of "traveling travel agent" to scour the countrysides, villages, and cities throughout Ireland, England, and central and eastern Europe.

And although Nikki had a secure life, the prospects for her future were not good, with few choices other than marrying into a family of means. So, it was one evening, while sitting around the table over plates of fried cabbage and kielbasa that Nikki spoke animatedly about an encounter she'd had in the city square.

"You'll not believe what I've heard, Papa!" she said. "And, Mama, you too! It was like church bells to me. There was a man dressed quite well in a three-piece suit with a starched white collar. He carried a satchel under his arm, and from it, he pulled a leaflet here and a leaflet there, handing them to anyone interested. I was, of course! And I took one. What would this man, in his accented, but perfect, Polish, have to say? He told us all to listen. That ships were regularly leaving from the harbor in Hamburg and sailing to America. He said the price would include a berth and two meals a day. And. . . Papa? It was not expensive. I, I. . . I have saved money from the ironing that I've taken in. . ." Her voice drifted. She studied her Papa's face, her Mama's, but there was no response. What did they make of it? They only looked at their empty plates, and the evening finished in silence.

A week went by, another week, and finally, Nikki's Papa said, "Come into the parlor, child. We must speak. I've discussed this matter with your mother. With prospects for this country going nowhere, and who knows where we'll end up, we believe you. It's with a heavy heart that you, a young woman, well-educated for a girl, should try your luck in America. You, who are so talented and industrious, I believe there, my dear girl, you will find your way in the world."

And so, in 1894 both Peter and Nikki left for America. The same year, from the same port on the North Sea. But they did not know one another. Not yet.

The journey by train from Warsaw took most of a day. The trip would have taken Nikki through the countryside of western Poland, Prussia, and eventually to the independent state of Hamburg.

For Peter, the message was much the same: Go to America where you can find a future. Traveling from rural Lithuania, the voyage took two days and 1,500 kilometers before reaching Cuxhaven, the port near Hamburg. With a cart and horse, his parents took him to Vilnius and dropped him off at the train station, knowing full well they would never see their son again. From there, Peter took the same journey as Nikki: through Poland and the Great Empire of Prussia along the coast of the North Sea, which until then was a place only dreamed of.

Between 1859 and 1934, over five million people left Europe for better opportunities in America. The famines, the wars, and the oppression of archaic rulers along with the promise of a life in which self-determination was the only obstacle standing in one's way, enticed even the poorest to leave. This huge influx of migrants suddenly invaded Hamburg, which caused a great problem for the local population. It seemed that overnight hordes of shabbily-dressed foreigners arrived, entire families in tow with wagons, babies, and bedding. They landed, stranded on the streets of the city, their life's savings sewn into the hems of skirts and the bottoms of trunks. There was nowhere to go until their ship took sail, which sometimes took days of waiting—perhaps it was the weather; perhaps it was cargo—but waiting left the desperate with no other means but to camp on the streets.

Albert Ballin had a solution for that, as well. Near Cuxhaven, Ballin erected some thirty buildings designed to accommodate these soon-to-be emigrants, a place where they were able to wait in comfort. Here they were given sleeping and living quarters and bathrooms. There was a dining hall where the travelers were fed two meals a day, and a music pavilion where they played their instruments, danced, and sang in all their native tongues. There was even a church and a synagogue.

After they departed, the journey took two weeks. For Nikki, it felt like a lifetime. She was seasick and in steerage, with no windows to tell whether another day had passed; she never knew where or how far they had come. Always there was the rocking. Adding to her fears (*I don't know the language. . . what foul man might approach me. . . what if I fail and don't find work?*), she thought surely she'd be sent back, just for being sick.

But in time, both Peter and Nikki arrived at Ellis Island, taking the final half-hour leg of the journey on a ferry from New York Harbor. The sight of the Statue of Liberty gave them chills. Hearts pounded beneath their clothing. Was it sunny that day? Cold? It was 1894.

Ellis Island was built only two years earlier. Over the next sixty years, more than twelve million immigrants would pass through its gates, full of hope in this land of promise.

Once they reached Ellis Island, the intake process took only a few hours. Doctors became proficient at the "Six-Second Inspection," assuming that passengers in first and second class would not be carrying diseases. Having traveled in steerage, however, Peter and Nikki needed full medical exams. After the exams, after all the stamping of official papers, agents would walk among the people, speaking all the European languages: Russian, Italian, German, Yiddish, and of course Lithuanian and Polish. Their job? Advise the newly-arrived immigrants where to go next. When it came to Peter, however, the official looking at his travel papers asked about his surname. "Mikolosius. It's your name?" he said in Polish, then in Russian.

"Da, da!" Peter answered. *Yes, yes!* What could be happening now? Now that he had already touched American soil (or brick, as it were).

"Mikolosius?" the inspector repeated. Then, in English with a ready translator by his side, he said, "Not advisable to keep that name, Sir. In America, we cannot pronounce it. Better to have an American name!" It was not only advised, it was required.

Peter, never having thought about this, asked, "What is a good name?"

"Well, I suggest you take your cue from the Irish. With a name like 'Mik,' sounds like 'Mc' to me."

"McLeish," cried a voice from behind. " 'Tis m'name, Sir, and you ken have all the right to it 'f ye'r willing. It'a make m'Da right proud!" The heavy Irish brogue was difficult even for the translator to understand.

So, there it was. The official wrote what he heard and from then on, Peter would be known by his new name, McLush, and Peter could not have been prouder. He was about to make a new life in this new country and changing his name was but a small first step.

The next step was walking up to the waiting agents who, upon hearing his language, advised him to go to Scranton, Pennsylvania. "There you'll find your people. And, more importantly? Plenty of work."

For Nikki, the process was not that different, although no one inquired about her surname. It was assumed she'd marry, and by marrying, her birth name would disappear anyway.

Each of them arrived by train in Scranton, alone and restless to find a footing, friends, a home, and work. For Peter, it was not difficult. The coal mines needed miners, and any young man, strong and willing to put in the time, was given a position.

Coal mining was not easy. Peter worked long hours, six days

a week, and in complete darkness with nothing but the carbide light emanating from his helmet. With an axe and chisel, he hammered away at chunks of coal, which were then placed in a cart that was pushed along rails to the daylight above. The world needed coal. It was how homes were heated, and how electricity was generated. You could say it was the lifeline of humanity. And the pay was solid, more than Peter ever dreamed of earning in Lithuania. His letters home were filled with exuberance.

For Nikki, there too was work. Scranton had ten textile factories, primarily producing lace and silk, and they offered plenty of machine jobs that could easily be handled by women. With her knowledge of all things sewing, mending, knitting, and crocheting, she landed a job quickly.

A typical day for both Peter and Nikki included a short lunch break. Nikki ate at her sewing machine while Peter sat on a rock inside the long, dark cave. But their hard work did not go unrewarded, as Sundays were for church, Saturday nights for pleasure.

It was on one of those Saturdays when Peter took to the local Polish pub for some lively music—a hand accordion and a fiddle playing what the immigrants loved most, the polka. And Peter knew well how to dance it. It took some energy, but that was something Peter had a lot of. He was strong, a large man with strong arms and legs to match. After ordering his pint and downing it, Peter looked around. A beautiful girl appeared from across the room.

Animatedly tapping her foot to the music, Nikki sat entranced. She wore her favorite and best clothes that night: a navy-blue belted dress and a white shawl. Her shoes were slightly scuffed, but had heels, not like the shoes she wore for work that were heavy and flat, the broken shoelaces tied into several knots. Her hair was pinned in a chignon, as was the fashion in the 1890s.

Peter watched her, intrigued, then turned to the man next to him and said, "Aleks? See that girl?"

"Yes," he replied, "She's beautiful."

"One day, Aleks, I tell you. . . I will marry her."

Nodding slyly with a twinkle in his eye, Peter gathered himself and walked over to Nikki, offering his hand with a slight bow, a gesture that asked, "Will you dance with me?"

Nikki, he learned quickly, was excellent at the polka. She knew steps and moves poor Peter could only try to emulate. Peter spoke a phrase in Polish, Nikki answered in Russian, and both laughed at their commonality and continued dancing until the last song of the night was announced.

Peter pursued her, wooed her, and danced with her through the next four years until Nikki finally said yes. In 1898, they married.

Peter stayed on as a coal miner. He was making a decent living and yet, as coal mining had it, he arrived home in the evenings dead-tired, face and hands so black with soot only the nail beds and the whites of his eyes shown through the grit. Wanting nothing more than a quick bowl of soup, he threw his tired body onto the bed he shared with Nikki, next to which sat a cradle, nearly always filled with a new baby.

Nikki never lost her passion for dancing though, and, with Peter's permission, she often took to the dance hall on Saturday nights with a few of her friends. Her joie de vivre never left her, right to the very end of her life.

Peter and Nikki found a balance in their lives. They lived in an apartment in Scranton where, over the next decade and a half, eight children were born, including a set of twins, although only one survived the birth. Then Peter started to have a terrible cough and soon became so short of breath that he could barely walk from the breakfast table to the door for work. It was assumed he had consumption, or TB, but Peter had something far worse—and incurable. He'd developed coal worker's pneumoconiosis, or "black lung disease." Eventually, he could no longer work.

In 1917, two years after their last child was born, Nikki took ill and died. A woman, working hard, long hours while bearing children every other year, often did not see her fourth decade in those times. Instead, death came far too soon, and, sadly, so it was for Nikki.

The firstborn was a boy named Wesley, an energetic, unpredictable child, who often caused his parents great concern. A fight at school, an upturned desk, extreme bouts of euphoria in which he spoke of angels and other mystical things, often refusing to eat or sleep. Then there were days and weeks in which he sullenly took to a corner of the house, not speaking to anyone. This difficult boy became a morose, and angry, teen.

The second-born was named Agnes. She was an easy child in comparison, never fussing and a delight to the family. Yet tragedy hit, as it did in many families those days. Agnes contracted polio when she was just three years old, a disease for which there was no cure and no vaccine (yet). Polio could stunt the growth of limbs, usually the legs, and this was so for Agnes. As a result, she walked with a limp for the duration of her life.

Even as a girl, Agnes was helpful in the home, caring for her siblings, in particular when new babies were born. She knew how to pin diapers, how to wash and hang them on the line. She knew how to cook their cereal, how to feed them, mend their stockings and patch the knees of their trousers, while Mother Nikolina did what she could to maintain the rest of the household.

Now Nikki was dead. And Peter, with his deep phlegm-filled cough, could no longer work. Agnes, the oldest of the girls, was expected to prepare the food, wash the clothes, and care for the younger ones while also keeping the house in order. Added to this was the grief of losing her mother. Finally, in desperation, she wrote to her relatives in Worcester, Massachusetts to ask for help. Agnes was fourteen.

There was no hesitation. Family takes care of family. So one clear morning, Agnes, with all six of her siblings and her ailing father, put those things they could carry into several trunks and made their way to the train station from which they rode the train three hundred miles east. Since his mother's death, Wesley had remained sullen and unable to help much. He sat alone at the rear of the train car the entire ride and refused to eat the sandwich Agnes had prepared for him. But no one paid attention. There was simply too much to hold in balance.

Wesley let his head sway to the rhythm of the train. Packing and leaving behind the only home he ever knew was one thing, but arriving at a completely new place, with new relatives in a house he did not know added to the uncertainty of it all. *How will we support ourselves? Where will our family go? What will happen to me?* He knew, as the oldest in the family, people should be able to rely on him.

Yet he was helpless.

It was only weeks then, after their arrival in eastern Massachusetts, that Wesley mysteriously died. To the family, Wesley was always "just a bit odd," and that's where the story stops. Suicide was something shameful to a family in those days. No one would dare even say the word. But it stands to reason half the sufferers of bipolar disorder attempt suicide, and for those with schizophrenia, the act is often successful. But we don't know for certain. And so Wesley is a relative whose history has gone with him to his grave.

In 1926, the family, including father Peter and all six remaining children, moved to an apartment in Sutton, Massachusetts, a small town with a small general store, a Baptist Church, and a sprinkling of surrounding farms. Agnes, now the oldest in the family and ever the resourceful one, found work at a stocking factory in Worcester. Each morning, Monday through Saturday, Agnes hobbled the mile to the bus stop, then rode an hour to her factory. At night, by the light of street lamps, she made her way home again. In this way, she was able to earn enough money to keep the family fed and clothed. She dedicated her young life to caring for her sickly father and younger siblings. But for her, there were still the Saturday nights.

GRANDPA OVID AND GRANDMA JOSEPHINE
Several Acres and a Brook That Ran Through It
CHARLTON, MASSACHUSETTS

Ovid, along with his brothers, helped Lewis on the farm. Margarette and the girls did the household chores. Money was never enough, though, and, as soon as he was old enough, Ovid went to work for the railroad. Here he managed the switching mechanisms to guide trains to and from the grand Union Station in Sutton, with its magnificent clock tower that still stands today.

His work took him to Springfield often. In this pleasant, quiet township, he would hop off the train to eat what his sisters had packed into his lunch pail: left-over meat pie, a biscuit or two, an apple, and always a thermos of steaming coffee.

One fragrant spring day in 1894, a pretty lady sat with her knitting on a neighboring bench in the Springfield station. On her head was a stylish hat that bobbed ever so slightly as she counted her stitches. Shyly Ovid smiled at her. Her name was Josephine. "Josephine Eudoxie Maynard is my name," is how she said it when he moved to take a seat next to her. "Eudoxie means 'comfort, good reputation,' and I have that," she said coyly. Then, in all seriousness, she repeated herself: " 'Josephine,' from the French. 'Eudoxie,' from the Greek. And 'Maynard' from everything else.' " At this, she giggled. Ovid was smitten.

Ovid and Josephine married a year later and settled on a small farm in Charlton. What Josephine lacked in height she made up for in kindness, and Ovid, like his parents, loved a house full of children. And over the next years, eight were born to them: Eva, Arthur, Peter. Chester in 1906. Then Raymond, Anita, Henry and Leo.

The farm had several acres with a brook running through it. Behind the farmhouse stood the long barn where a few cows and a lone muscular workhorse lived. The hay to feed them in winter was kept dry in the hayloft above their stalls. Not far from the kitchen's backdoor was a chicken coop, and beside it a small fenced-in pen for the pigs. This made it easy for Josephine and the girls to run the food scraps out while they were cooking. Beyond the pigpen was a large plot where the family garden was planted each spring: potatoes, corn, cucumbers for pickles, okra, carrots, turnips, and greens (collard, spinach, kale, and dandelion—a plant brought over from England in the 1600s and considered a staple, as good for nutrition as it was medicinal). And there, behind the long barn, was a pasture full of grass and wildflowers so tall it could tickle a five-year-old's ears. Apple trees dotted the front yard, creating a dust barrier to the road. Josephine was famous for her apple pies, apple fritters, apple sauce, and just about anything else "apple," including the glaze for hams she baked at Christmastime.

Ovid and Josephine owned two wagons: One for work, the other for transport, mainly to go to church. The children walked to school, which was a one-room building with a front door, a back door, and a potbelly stove. Eight rows of desks filled the interior—two rows for each of the four grades. The desks were wooden benches attached to desks with tops that flipped up to expose everything a student needed: a slate, a slate pencil, a cloth to wipe the slate clean, a sandwich, and a handkerchief. After each lesson, the slates were erased, making it necessary to memorize everything.

Mrs. Fields was the teacher. She nearly always stood at the front of the room where a large black swivel board stood tall by her side. Only when she needed to discipline did she move about, up and down the rows to make sure no one was cheating, or sleeping. Each week a different child filled the firewood box in the morning. The job was always given to the boys. The girls received their moniker, "teacher's pet," because, invariably, they were the ones who made sure the coats were hung properly, the dictionary put away neatly—anything to be on Mrs. Fields' good side. Having their knuckles rapped, as the boys so often had, was not something they were about to experience. Rapt attention was the better avenue, and the girls knew how to at least fake it.

Behind Mrs. Fields, behind her slate board, in either corner of the room, were the entrances to the boys' and girls' coatrooms. Inside each coatroom was a narrow door that opened into a sort of indoor outhouse with three cutouts on a wooden platform that made for three toilets. For toilet paper, torn pieces of newspaper lay at the side of each cutout. Hands were not washed; there was no running water. This was left for that time "before supper" and usually done at the pump outside the farmhouse and at home.

While the boys in Ovid and Josephine's family worked the farm, providing most or even all the food the family needed— eggs, vegetables, fruit, meat, bacon—Ovid continued to work for the railroad, giving the family the little extra cash they needed to pay the rent and buy the necessaries, fabric, and farm tools. In time, the oldest son, Arthur, joined his Pa at the railroad. Yes, you could say they had it good, but with all that, the money never seemed to reach the end of the month. Finally, at the age of eleven, Chester (Chet), too, quit school to help.

Chet could do anything—build things and fix things. He knew machinery, he knew farming, he knew animals. He tried his hand at butchering, then painted houses for a while. He knew what people needed and wanted. He even started a trucking company once that delivered goods, milk, and hay to people's doorsteps. But he never returned to school. His formal schooling had lasted five years. The rest of what he knew was life's lessons, and that was a lot.

It wasn't all work for Chet, though. He knew how to take time off for himself, too. Every Saturday he went to his favorite dance hall with bands whose players were mostly the local farmers playing fiddles, banjos, accordions. "Swing your ladies, do-si-do. . ." Worcester, being a large city in comparison to the farm town of Charlton, held the best square dances with musicians from all parts of the state. Here, in 1926, three years before the financial crash that rocked the world, Chet met the most beautiful woman he'd ever laid eyes on. Her name was Agnes McLush.

DAD CHET AND MA AG
The Business

Like her mother, Agnes loved the dances, even though she insisted "I don't dance, thank you very much." Yet that night, in her pretty shoes and tiny feet, a full-skirted dress and jacket to match, she held her hands clasped against her cheeks, tantalized by the moves the couples made on the dance floor. Chet, ever interested in a dance partner, walked over and asked her to dance. Bashfully, she shook her head, no thank you. But Chet seemed to have missed the cue, because he took her hand in his and led her to the center of the floor. It was then that he noticed the slight limp in her stride. He deftly, and gently, showed her a few very simple-to-follow moves. But he did not want to break her, her beautiful timidity, and asked if she preferred to sit. To this she happily exclaimed, yes.

"She's still as beautiful as she was at seventeen," he'd say when asked about that night. And she would say, "There he was, walking across the room. I thought he couldn't be coming to talk to me. But he was coming to talk to me. And he said, I'm Chet. At that moment I knew. I just knew."

Chet and Agnes, called "Ag" by those who loved her, married in 1927, then moved to Oxford, to an apartment where Agnes's sister Rose, her two brothers, and her widowed father Peter lived. Here their first child, Phyllis, was born right in the apartment. A doctor made the house call.

A year later, black lung disease finally took Peter's life. It was 1928, a year before the terrible crash, and a second child was on the way. It would be a son this time, Chester, Jr., born in Worcester MA in 1929.

By now Chet was fully employed as a self-made house painter, and business was booming. Everyone wanted what Chet could do so well. He painted houses, he painted trim, he painted interiors, bathrooms, and parlors. People relished the new-found freedom that came with the 1920s. "Live a little," they'd upbraid one another, and so Chet and Agnes picked up their family and moved once more, this time to Charlton, further west in Massachusetts, where customers were abundant. Entire neighborhoods of once dingy clapboard houses blossomed into neat rows of blue, lavender, green, ochre, and rose, with stark trims in orange, gray, charcoal, and maroon.

Another year and another child: Paul. It was now 1931. The stock market had finally crashed. Although no one knew it was the Depression—that name came much later—business began to dwindle. Mortgages dried up. Banks foreclosed on homes and farms, as they, too, were short on funds. Chet's clients stopped needing, or wanting, home improvements. Painting could easily wait for better times.

Since prehistory, humans have covered their living quarters with art. The earliest images date to 30,000 years ago, when, it is believed, cave paintings were first made to tell a story—of a hunt, of a family. Every continent in the world, with the exception of Antarctica, has remnants of cave art. Is it possible these humans also simply wanted to decorate their homes?

The Egyptians took mural painting to another level, adorning their tombs with stories that stretched from royalty to slavery. Later, the Greeks, Minoans, and ultimately the Romans expounded upon the art, creating intricate frescos such as those at Pompeii. As wools, linens and silks from China became more available, tapestries started to cover walls. The most famous of these is the Bayeux tapestry, which stretches 236 feet and depicts the Norman Conquest of England. The history of that war in 1066 is told scene by scene, embroidered with wool thread on linen cloth and now hangs in the Bayeux Museum in Normandy, France.

The Chinese are credited with putting art on rolls of paper, finally allowing even the working class the ability to adorn their walls. And Chet took advantage of that. He could paper an entire room in the time it would take just to tape it off for painting. Armed with a catalogue of wallpaper samples that showcased hundreds of patterns, some flocked (using left-over scraps from cut silk), some with whimsical floating frying pans and cowboys, some merely highlighting a certain color, Dad traveled from house to house, teaching the housewives how to reinvent their homes. Once again, Dad's business boomed.

BOB

The General Store on Richardson's Corner

1934–1939

This is where I come in.

The apartment on Fox Street in Worcester, where my parents and three older siblings lived when I was born March 18, 1934, was typical for a city dwelling: Two apartments stacked one above the other. Our apartment was the one on the main level, so our front door was the first thing you saw upon entering the foyer. This front door led into our living room where a large, patterned rug covered the hardwood floor. An overstuffed couch with purple velvet upholstery sat in the middle of the room facing the fireplace; to the left, and the front of the house, there were two large bay windows with benches beneath, a hulking, clanging radiator off to one corner.

I was now three, no longer needing to sit in the highchair as that was taken up by baby Patricia. I was old enough to sit on a real chair with a phone book under me, and old enough to know something important was being discussed. Dad came to the table that night all aflush. He'd been approached by one of his clients, a man named Tom, who was selling a piece of property. "I think you'd be interested in this, Chet," he said. "It sounds right up your alley. It's a small grocery store, but don't jump to conclusions. Not yet. The location can't be beat. You know that intersection at Route 20 that runs all the way to Boston? That corner they call 'Richardson's Corner'?"

Chet wasn't speaking, but he wasn't distracted either. He just kept looking at Tom, who understood it to mean he should keep talking. "Yeah, you know that corner all right. There's a store there, for sale. It's my store. You'd do well running something like that, Chet. Think about it."

Chet stared bewildered. "I mean, Tom. How would I do that? I mean, with the kids and all?"

Tom reached over and put his hand on Chet's. "I know you, Chet. I know you've got a work ethic that's unmatched. And you want to get out of the wall-business at some point, don't you? Well, think on it. It's not going anywhere."

This was pretty much the same speech Dad gave at dinner that night. I studied Ma's face. After all, she was the one who wore the pants in the family. Nothing was decided without her blessing. Dad mused, "How convenient would that be? All the traffic going east and west drives right by it. Suppose someone needs a Coke? Some borax powder or oil for the engine?"

Ma said something then that surprised me. She didn't say yes or no; she didn't even ask questions. She just said, "Chet. I've some money saved," and rose from the table. She went to the kitchen and reached for a high shelf, pulling down a tea tin that she'd tucked well behind a box of Post Toasties Corn Flakes. "I think we can do this, Chet. I've been putting money away since nearly the time I knew you. Since 1927."

It was all Dad needed to hear, and from then on the house was aflutter with activity. Being only three, I didn't know about mortgages and down payments and all. I'm sure that was arranged, but it seemed no time at all until we were suddenly living in a house. A real house. No more neighbors above us. No more yelling, "Keep it down. The neighbors will pound!" Now we had a yard with plenty of room to play. Here was another exciting thing: I was going to start school in the very same schoolhouse Dad had attended, with the very same teacher, Mrs. Fields.

I discovered that everything Dad had said about that schoolhouse was true. The potbelly stove, the toilets with the cutouts, the desks with tops that lifted. There was an inkwell, now, and real toilet paper, but Mrs. Fields looked exactly the way I'd pictured her: stout, no nonsense, her hair combed into a severe bun. The one thing Dad never told me that I think he should have is how it smelled in that one-room school. Full of sour milk and manure. And the girls! They often had hay still stuck to their sweaters, and there was not a single boy whose fingernails were clean. I looked at my own nails and confirmed this to be true. But this was small-town life, and I was now a part of it.

Two bedrooms were upstairs in our new house: one where the girls slept, one where the boys slept. Ma and Dad slept downstairs. There was no furnace where we slept, only a hole in the floor with a grate over it, where supposedly heat from the stove below would creep in. This was not always the case, though. Winter mornings often saw the water glass at the side of my bed, frozen.

I knew we didn't have money. I knew things were different from the time before. But I wasn't around during the time before. I was around now, and that meant, for me, everything was a hand-me-down. New trousers, even for church, just didn't happen. Ma patched our clothes, and I was the third in a line of boys whose jeans and boots I could just as well wear as not.

The step from the back door landed on a well-worn path

that led directly to the side entrance of the store, no more than thirty feet away. A kitchen window was right there, too, so that Ma or Aunt Rose could see when a car pulled up and we had a customer. Ma, or Aunt Rose, would grab the baby, put her in a handheld cradle and trot over to attend to business. Baby Patricia watched the goings on from the viewpoint of her cradle, set atop a crate of bread or a couple cases of beers.

Route 20, a lone asphalt streak across the state, was cobblestone right where our store was. I could hear the cars coming before I saw them. There was that *ba-boomp, ba-boomp* when they drove by, but when the noise slowed down—more like *ba-boooooomp*—it was all the announcement we needed to walk over to see what they wanted. Me being me, I loved those moments, because I could "shop" to my heart's content. No one paid me much attention when there were customers. Beside the Campbell's soups, Borden's milk, and cans of Spam, was a glassed-in candy case near the cash register. It was open from the back, and when no one was watching, I took my chances. I reached in and grabbed some of that penny candy. Red strands of licorice, bubble-gum cigars, Tootsie Rolls, Bazooka gum with the funnies wrapped inside, and all this fit nicely inside my trouser pockets. And I could easily play the smart guy and help out when I was needed, showing people where to find the cigarettes and what-not.

Dad still catered to a few of his good clients, always driving off in the mornings with his catalogue of wallpaper and fabric samples. Sometimes he took me with him on Saturdays when all he needed to do was clean up. He'd ask me to take a bucket and walk around, picking up scraps and loading them in the truck. "We don't want to leave a mess behind, makes them not want to tell their neighbors about me. Gives me a bad reputation," he counseled.

What Happened in September 1938

It was 1938, September 21. I woke up to a sky that was greenish. I'll never forget it, that grayish green. The air was perfectly still—no birds, no barking dogs—and my mother said, "Bobby. I want to take you shopping."

One thing my mother loved was shopping, particularly for bargains. It was something she learned early on in life, when her mother's sudden death made her the new matron by default. Today, it was Wednesday. Phyllis, Chet (who we called Sonny now), and Paul were all at school. Ma figured Aunt Rose could take care of the baby and also manage the store. And here I was, four years old, with nothing much else to do, and my mom wanted to spend a day with just me. It felt so very special.

Dad drove the two of us into Worcester and dropped us off at Ware Pratt, a department store for boy's and men's clothes, one of Ma's favorites.

"Did you feel that?" Ma asked as we crossed the street. "Did you feel a raindrop?" I did, but I was too excited to care. "I think it's going to rain. Better get inside!" And so, we hurried on.

We looked at everything, up to the next floor and the next, finally taking the elevator back down, one of my other favorite things to do. The elevator doors were made of ornate wrought-iron that were clanged shut by a uniformed man who worked a wheel that looked much like the steering wheel on Dad's big truck. Soft orchestral music played in the background. Ma said, "Main floor, please."

We then went to Denholm & McKay's and ended up at Filene's. I don't recall Ma buying anything, maybe she did, maybe she bought some cloth for a dress for Phyllis or for her, but, more importantly, she had her sights set on the Warner's Theater on Front Street. It was owned by Warner Brothers in Hollywood, which made it a fancy theater, and on this day, they were showing a double-feature, a musical, and Ma loved the musicals. So, after looking at all the bargains, after riding the elevator up and down, and after lunching at the Woolworth's (I ordered my favorite, meatloaf, mashed potatoes, and a slice of apple pie), Ma and I walked over to the theater. Fred Astaire and Ginger Rogers were dancing in a film titled *Carefree*. The grand entrance and the plush velvet seat that leaned back when I pushed my feet against the chair in front were nothing but spectacular. But the best part was, all the while, I got to be with my Ma. Just me and my Ma.

Three hours of movies passed. I didn't want it to end. But it was getting late in the afternoon. Dad, who'd had to work in Worcester that day, was waiting for us outside. As we passed through the cinema doors, fat raindrops splashed loudly on the sidewalk. With heads bent, we ran into the street and hurried into the cab of the truck, shaking the water out of our hair.

"Holy Toledo!" Dad exclaimed watching his windshield wipers unsuccessfully move the water from one side to the other. What little he could see was but through a blur.

I remembered a news report had come on the radio that morning on our drive into town. Ma and Dad didn't make much of it, but I heard them say a hurricane might hit the coast later in the day. Well, Worcester was inland, so we didn't really have much to worry about.

Wipers beating fast the whole way, it took us two-and-a-half hours to drive the fifteen miles back to our home. Every road Dad tried was blocked with downed trees, downed telephone poles and wires, abandoned cars, the siding from a house. We knew nothing. We worried only that Aunt Rose and baby Patricia would worry. That, and of course, did the kids make it home from school okay? There were no phone booths along the way, and with all the downed telephone poles, the chance of getting a call through were nil. We just had to make it home. We drove back roads with little to no houses, hoping that if something was downed, it was not going to be lying all over the street.

It was dusk by the time we got home. Being too excited about the rain, I did not help Ma with dinner as usual. Instead, I put on my swim trunks and ran outside. This was simply too exciting! Rain and rain and water everywhere. The entire yard between the house and the store was one big lake. With giant steps I splashed through it, back and forth. When the wind gusted so hard it felt like it could blow me over I grew stronger and, with clenched fists and head bowed, I marched forward.

Big things happened in September: 9/11. Germany invaded Poland. And here was this: the worst hurricane ever to hit the United States—a story that filled newspapers across the country and around the world for weeks to come. By the time it was over, the entire coastline of Connecticut, Rhode Island, and Massachusetts was destroyed. Twenty-five thousand homes and businesses, gone. Seven hundred people lost their lives. Stories were told of chicken coops being lifted and dropped a hundred feet away, not a chicken dead, not an egg cracked. Cars with people inside found dead, hands still on the steering wheel. There was no satellite, no televised weather report, not even a functioning weather tracking system. No one was prepared. The damages would cost $306 million—six and a half billion in today's dollars.

A year later, you could still see the damage, but people were flocking to the beaches again. The boardwalks, cafés, and shops were back and functioning, and anyway, for us, there were those Saturdays when Dad wanted nothing more than to spend the day with the family and go to the beach. Ma seemed to know when those Saturdays came about, because she was always already up making peanut butter and jelly sandwiches, wrapping up some chicken salad, and stirring up a couple of envelopes of Kool-Aid to bring. We had a small wicker picnic basket that held all our plates and forks, checked napkins, and a checked tablecloth. This, too, she packed into the back of the Chevrolet along with a tote full of fruit—bananas, apples, and grapes. In the front seat sat Dad (the driver), Ma at the right-hand door, and me on the bench seat between them. Phyllis stayed home with Aunt Rose to watch baby Patricia, but here's what really got my goat. The Chevrolet was a 1937 coup, no backseat, that my Dad had borrowed from his brother, my uncle Henry. That coup had a rumble seat, and guess who got to sit in it? My two older brothers, Sonny and Paul. I wanted so badly to sit there, but I was too young. "You'll slide off when we take a corner. And then what? You gonna walk home?" It was enough to scare me, but it didn't take away the fact that I was jealous. That rumble seat sure looked neat. Tan tufted leather. I'll never forget it.

There were many beaches Dad liked to take us to: Narragansett Pier, Point Judith, Cape Cod. And, sometimes, some special times, we went all the way to Crescent Park in East Providence with its daringly high roller coaster built of wood with a metal track, a gigantic (by my standards) carousel with a spectacularly loud hand organ, hand-carved wooden horses and a brass ring that, if you caught it when the carousel rounded by, you'd win yourself a free ride. Crescent Park had a world-famous shore dinner hall, too, that seated 2,000 people. Imagine that! Two thousand people, all eating clam chowder, clam cakes, buttered corn on the cob, watermelon, even lobster, all at the same time.

But today was not a day for Crescent Park. We were going down the road to Narragansett Pier to picnic and swim. It was about one and three-quarters hours' drive, timing it early enough, Dad figured, to catch the beach at low tide. That gave us a good seven more hours for fun. Needless to say, it was exciting. The cobblestone road, the full-on highway, then, suddenly, the smell of seawater, and finally the sight of the ocean with its noisy, powerful waves. I immediately forgot all about that rumble seat and challenged my brothers to a race to the water's edge. I was five now and knew, if I called it while getting a head start running, there was a chance, always a chance, that I might win.

Paul and Sonny chased after me, and, as I recall, I did win. But we had more important things to do. We had seashells to collect. Sonny and Paul had pails ready for this venture and told me to wait, they'd be back in half an hour. I didn't care. I had my own reasons. I wanted to dig myself a trench and lay down in the cool sand.

And so, I started digging with my little spade, not getting very far, because water kept filling up my hole. Finally, my brothers arrived to see what I was doing. Their tin pails were now full and I was curious. "Whatcha got there, Sonny? Can I see?"

"You can see, but you can't touch. These are valuable things. They're real seashells."

"Ooooh. They're beautiful." I wanted so badly to touch one, but then Sonny said he'd help me with the trench idea.

"C'mon, Bobby! Help me dig!" he said. I forgot all about the shells and we got busy making a hole that looked like a box for dead people. Sonny told me it was called a casket. I'd seen pictures before. We dug and dug and then Paul climbed in it. We buried him, right up to his chin. Only his face showed and he looked like a mummy, rolling his eyes in the back of his head, like he might have been a real dead person. He sure made us laugh. The tide was coming in. One wave, a few more. Another wave and slowly his sand mummy-sack melted away. "I'm gonna getcha!" Paul screamed, jumping out to beat us both to the blanket where Ma had our picnic ready under a beach umbrella.

After lunch, I took off with my brothers, all of us holding our pails. We had a new idea. We were going to meet the neighbors. Coca-Cola bottles, back then, were worth two cents each, paid as a deposit that was refunded when returning the empties. But here we were on the beach and there were plenty of folks around that, we noticed, were drinking Cokes. "Let's get some money!" Sonny exclaimed, and I was all for it. Especially since my two big brothers were in on it, too. By walking up to people as they lay on their beach blankets, it was not hard to ask, as a polite young man, if they happened to have any empties they'd like us to take off their hands. Most everyone we met was a willing business partner in our enterprise, and I was able to collect eighteen bottles; all I needed to do was give them to Ma who'd just hand them off to the Coke delivery man. That was not a bad day of work. Thirty-six cents, all for me, when a movie only cost a dime, and penny candy was still only a penny. I was a pride-filled sight. Maybe I could do this as a living one day. I had that sort of charm, I figured. Just like my Pa. With good manners and a kindly smile, why you could go places.

Our outing at Narragansett Pier that day could be considered a success. No wind, tons of sun and fun, but the tide was coming in and the sun was dimming—both signs we had to go home. We loaded our gear into the car. Sonny and Paul sat in the rumble seat again. Sonny read his comic books while Paul looked through his assortment of seashells, throwing out those that were broken or not so pretty. Then, with one last endearing wave goodbye to the sea, Paul's blue wide-brimmed cap, a cap he never went without, flew off into the high sky, never to be seen again.

3

Again, a New Home, Again a New Language

 URSULA

EUROPE, 1938–1939

JUNE 8, 1938

> A new law prohibits Hitler Youth from eating ice cream while in uniform.

JUNE 9, 1938

> Bombs explode in twenty-seven mailboxes and two post offices in England. Seven people are injured.

JUNE 9, 1938

> The oldest synagogue of Munich is destroyed.

On June 9, 1938, the Deutschland Tour completed its final stage. The cyclists had ridden over 1,500 kilometers in six days and were now finishing in Berlin. My Papa was among them. He'd been an athlete competing in international distance and Velodrome races for many years and was famous among the fans. Handsome, strong, and rich, he moved in the world as if he owned it.

When I think of my Papa, I remember the smell of leather and his cologne. I remember the soft lambs' wool in his Horch, how it felt against my bare feet. I remember the colors: the pale, blush-yellow leather, the lambswool floor like butter cream. Mami's winter-sky blue chiffon skirt that billowed with the slightest breeze. Then I remember Mami's tight curls and her pearl earrings, me in the backseat with the top down.

August 1, 1938

> The State government in Nazi Germany and Austria declares all unions between people of "different blood" illegal. "From this day hence, such couples are to divorce in order to prohibit the reproduction of the inferior race."

August 3, 1938

> Italy bans immigrant Jewish children from attending school.

A Beguiling Birthday

I was born Ursula Luisa Krehn on August 6, 1934, in Berlin, Germany.

It was a Saturday on August 6 when I turned four. I remember the morning, fresh with chirping birds and sunlight glinting through the tall leaves above. I remember the wicker picnic basket and the wine glasses—three: one for Papa and Mami each, and one for me. Our house girl, Klara, packed a bottle of raspberry juice and said it was special wine just for me. Because, she said, it was my birthday.

Papa dressed for the seaside in a white polo shirt and white linen trousers, his pencil mustache freshly waxed, his wavy hair pomaded into a neat dovetail at his neckline. I remember his broad hands as he squatted and reached for me. "*Komm, meine Ursula!*" he said. "We're going to the seashore!" Papa was always aflutter when we went on an excursion. His 1933 Horch 830 was brought early that morning from the warehouse, sparkling in the morning dew.

I remember walking under the rows of plane trees that led from our villa to the shore on the Wannsee. My Papa held my hand like it was his tennis ball. I remember looking down the beach and seeing the Strandbad, the open-air lido with all the people bathing, and the blue-striped umbrellas. I remember wishing a bottle with a message just for me would wash onto the sand.

Mami spread the picnic blanket on the shore and pulled the glasses, plates, and silver from the wicker basket.

"To another summer of excellent business, excellent wine, and a beautiful wife." Papa's eyes twinkled as he clinked his glass against Mami's, winking at me, toasting my glass and then winking again. Papa owned a store for fancy men, not as big as Grandpapa Sally's, but it was fancy all the same. Hats and leather gloves and silver cigarette cases and cigarette holders made of ivory.

Papa had ideas about the store that Mami and Tantes Hanni and Gerda and Grandmama Martha inherited. Business was not going well for them, they were discovering. Ever since Grandpapa Sally died a year ago, things were falling apart.

Grandpapa Sally was my Mami's Papa. He was rich and stern and always carried a large black umbrella that he used as a walking stick. His bowler-shaped hat was old-fashioned, but elegant. After his death, the business of running the department store landed upon the shoulders of the four women in his life—Gerda, Hanni, my Mami Eleanor, and Grandmama Martha. This was not the best situation. First, they were women, never taught to run a business, and they were elegant women, never expected to run a business, let alone a giant "Kaufhaus" with its lavishly decorated shops and cafés, all bright and airy. There is one more reason I will soon tell you about, a reason neither Papa nor Mami quite knew about yet.

"But Hans," Mami answered soberly that day on the beach. "Berlin is in such chaos. Not only have the customers stopped, but Ilse and Lieselotte, Hanni's very good friends, will no longer visit. They say it's not safe. What can come of this?"

Papa shook his head at her. "Ach, Eleanor. You worry, my darling. You worry too much."

I remember the disappearing sun that evening, the redness over the lake, the stillness. It was the last time I would see the villa. The last time we would drive in that Horch, the long sleek cabriolet with an extra tire, spokes and all, attached to the side.

AUGUST 10, 1938

The Grand Synagogue of Nuremberg is destroyed.

AUGUST 17, 1938

Nazi Germany requires all Jews bearing first names of non-Jewish origin to adopt an additional name: "Israel" for men and "Sara" for women.

SEPTEMBER 1, 1938

All Jews who entered Italy as of January 1, 1919 are ordered to leave within six months.

SEPTEMBER 2, 1938

Italy orders all Jewish teachers, officials, and students be expelled from state schools.

NOVEMBER 7, 1938

A German diplomat is shot in front of the Embassy in
Paris by a disgruntled man whose Jewish parents were
among those deported from Germany to Poland.

Everything is So New

A somber mood descended over our house not long after that
day at the Wannsee. Papa still left in the mornings and came
home in the afternoons, usually with a surprise for me in his
pocket, and Mami still did as she always did. Still, we shopped
for things like shoes and a chandelier. And we always had nougat
Torte at the Kafé Kranzler. We ate our Abendbrot in the parlor
each evening. But things felt gray. I could not put words to it, but
worry flourished in every room.

Then one day, the bubble burst, and this is the third thing I
want to tell you about: Grandpapa's big store. Papa came home
nearly right after he left that morning, his coffee still warm in
his cup. "Eleanor," he stated as if it was a sentence unto itself.
"Pack up. I'm taking you to the Kurfürstendamm. Ursula? You
are to come too. You must see this for yourselves."

Nothing could have prepared me for what I saw there.
Only the motion pictures could describe it, and then not even
accurately. Grandpapa's store was where we went first. The
shop-windows around the entire store—and it was a very big
store that took a whole block and several streetlights to walk
all the way around—were broken; all of them. Papa said it had
happened sometime in the night. He said it was the SS, a new
term I had not heard. They must be very, very bad people; who
would do such a thing?

Signs with red and black letters hung in the empty spaces

where windows had been. I could read a little of what was written there. Klara had taught me. She had also shown me things like question marks and exclamation points. It was fun drawing these: a line, a squiggly line, a dot underneath. Now, here I saw that exclamation point over and over. Klara told me it meant when someone shouted, or it was really, really important. But here I saw three in a row: *Deutsche!!!* I knew, too, the word, *Jude.* I just did not know what it was, exactly. I thought it meant, "rich person," because every time we drove through big neighborhoods with big estate houses, the comment the adults so often made was, *"Das sind wohl Juden"*—those must be Jews.

All along the Ku-damm, as Berliners affectionately called the avenue as grand as the Champs Elysée in Paris, the hotels, restaurants, car showrooms, every place had its windows broken. A small shop, so fancy it could have been my Papa's, had three placards hanging in the empty windows. Each placard yelled, "Jude!" "Jude!" "Jude!" I did not know what to make of all this. Glass everywhere, everyone scurrying like a storm was about to hit. I was frightened. My Mami looked frightened, too. She shushed me and rushed me and said emphatically, "Come, child! You've seen too much. At least your Papa's shop is still safe."

NOVEMBER 9, 1938

Named Kristallnacht, Jewish establishments and synagogues across Germany are looted and destroyed in retaliation for the assassination of Ernst vom Rath in Paris. Twenty thousand Jews are arrested.

There were big changes—and constant hushed conversations— at home after that day. Klara was let go. That was the first big change. Papa no longer took out his Horch, or any of his collection of German-made cars, for that matter: the Mercedes, the Opel Admiral, the BMW. He preferred the S-Bahn, now, to go to work. Mami wrung her hands often, pressing the fingers of her left hand through the fingers of her right. She used the telephone nearly daily to speak with her sisters, Hanni and Gerda. "I'm not understanding this. I'm just not understanding this at all." An hour later the phone would ring and it was always Tante Hanni or Tante Gerda. And Mami would say it all over again.

Grandmama was now blind. Some say it was the pneumonia that took her eyesight. Some say she may have had tuberculosis. What I say is she didn't want to see anymore. I mean, look at what happened to her, to her store, to her family.

Then Grandmama Martha moved in with Tante Hanni. It was the best solution.

November 12, 1938

All Jewish-owned businesses in Germany are permanently closed by the "Decree on the Exclusion of Jews from German Economic Life."

November 12, 1938

All Jews in Germany are ordered to pay a collective fine of 1 billion Reichsmarks for the murder of Ernst vom Rath. Each Jew in possession of property over 50,000 RM is required to pay 20 percent of its value.

November 15, 1938

All Jewish children are banned from German public schools.

November 15, 1938

Italy orders all books by Jewish authors be removed from schools.

Not a Time for Questions

Papa rushed in the door middle of the day, too early for the shop to have closed. He phoned earlier, and after that call, Mami was distracted and wrung her hands even more, often pushing her hair back, a nervous gesture I knew to mean, "Don't talk to me now." Her eyes flitted as she spoke through pressed lips, "Put Genevieve into your suitcase. We're going with Papa. Go now. Do as I say."

I knew not to ask. Questions were for later when Mami was like this, but I peered out from behind my playroom door, observing what she did next. Next were three large travel trunks sitting at the door, the same door my Papa burst through only twenty minutes later. I was allowed one toy, my Käthe Kruse doll, Genevieve, the most trusted companion I now had.

"*Dein Pass?*" he hurriedly asked.

"*Ja, ja,*" my Mami answered.

"*Das Silber? Das Gold?*"

"*Ja, Hans. Ja, alles!*"

It was as if a wind had swept in and carried us in one giant gust to the waiting taxi in the circular drive. "To the train station," Papa demanded through pressed lips, pulling a handful of Reichsmarks from his jacket pocket, held as though he never wanted to touch those coins again. I turned back to peer through the rear window one last time. I watched the house and the linden tree grow smaller. The neighbor's dog stood barking. Then the hill disappeared everything. It would be the last I saw of our home on Grünewald Strasse.

We arrived at the train station and as we exited the taxi, Mami squatted down to see me and smiled. She brushed the hair from my forehead and said, "Nothing to worry for. . . We're going on holiday. And you'll learn Italian! It's the most beautiful language! Like music to the ear."

All throughout our train ride, Papa read his paper while Mami taught me words—*buongiorno* and *buonasera*—and sentences like "*Che belle le montagne*" as the train took us through the Alps. Mami was a master at languages. She was very smart and had a degree in foreign language studies. She knew everything about Italian.

It was a luxury train with a Pullman dining car, white linen tablecloths, and servers wearing white gloves with a large serviette flipped over a bent arm. I was allowed an Eis Becher, a silver cup with vanilla ice cream, a sugar wafer sticking out the top. Best of all, I didn't even need to finish my potatoes and beef. This was already a very fine holiday. Mami looked stunning in her red lipstick and tapered wool suit. She told me then a little of what had happened.

"Tante Hanni and Onkel Werner are on a train now, too. And Grandmama Martha. They're traveling to England! Think about that. They have a real king there!"

"Oh!" I said, "I want to visit!"

"Yes. Surely, we can. But here's more news. Your Tante Gerda and Onkel Harry are traveling even farther away. To China!"

"China? Is it where they make the vases from Ming?" It was the only reference I had to that place. I did not even know it was a place. I only knew that the two vases as tall as me and painted in delicate blues were vases I was not to touch. Ever. Klara told me this. "They are valuable and from the Ming dynasty," she said earnestly, one day as she was dusting.

I wasn't even sure I wanted an answer. What I really wanted to know was how long this holiday would last. It seemed we'd been on the train for an awful long time, and I had my friends Frieda back home, and Heidi. I hadn't properly said goodbye.

After a night spent in a sleeping car and a breakfast with many cheeses and Wurst and toasted bread and jam, the train finally came to a stop. Papa was dressed in his dapper way, and Mami wore a flared dress with large front pockets and a leather belt, a fur coat over it. I had on my shiny black patent leather buckle shoes and a tweed coat with a matching hat that had pom-poms that tied under my chin. I thought we looked rather magnificent as we surely should, stepping off in this new country.

Papa had arranged a lovely yet small apartment for us in Milan. It was furnished, but only sparsely. I wondered about that. Our home and the villa had so many rugs and cushions, photographs and paintings. This home had none of that.

As soon as Papa unlocked the door, as soon as the driver brought in our three trunks, as soon as we stood in the vestibule, coats still on, Mami squatted before me so we were eye-to-eye. Her hands clutched both my little arms, and she said, "*Du musst jetzt brav sein.*"—you need to be well-behaved now.

I understood this new place was important. "But, how long, Mami? What about my toys and books that are still at home?" I felt tears well up that I didn't want her to see. I wanted to be *brav*, as she had asked, and so I quickly wiped them away with the backs of my hands.

"Not very long, my darling. Not long. . ." Mami stopped talking as though she was thinking what more to say. Then she stroked my cheek and said, "Long enough for you to learn Italian!"

This gave me encouragement. I was always up for learning. Already I knew to say, "*Che bella*" and "*Grazie.*" I was satisfied. At least for the time being.

Our days took on a routine. Papa had work, but it was different from that in Berlin. In Berlin, he was "Herr Kaufmann," the businessman who took care of his shop and employees and brought home treats. Now he was "*Signore Professore.*" He no longer came home in the middle of the day to go for an afternoon train ride, or to take us for a drive to the countryside. Now he was gone after his coffee and cheese bread in the morning until it was already suppertime. Papa had a position at the university teaching first-year students German. A prestigious position, Mami told me. Not all Germans were able to get work.

Mami stayed home with me. We took long walks together. She would point to things and say them in Italian. I was to repeat and then try to put a sentence to it. Window, mannequin, hat. Tree, leaves, street. I learned cannoli, gelato, and pizza and would recite at night to both my Papa and my Mami what all I'd learned that day.

More and more Papa and Mami talked in hushed voices long after our evening meal, long after I was sent to bed. Things were not exactly right, but I could not discern what they were. They both said to me and to each other, "It won't be long," which was getting to be repetitive, and I was beginning to sense it was nowhere near the truth.

One evening at the table I wanted a definitive answer. Knowing my Papa liked a good joke, I asked it like this: "Papa? I have a riddle for you."

"Ja?" he asked. "I'm always up for a riddle! What is it?"

"What keeps coming and coming and coming but never arrives?"

"I don't know, *mein kind*. What keeps coming and coming and coming and never arrives?"

"Tomorrow!" I giggled behind my hands. It was so funny to me.

But Papa looked astonished. He turned to Mami and said, "She's brilliant, this child. She'll go places one day."

It's Official

A time came when Papa announced something big. He wanted Mami and me to be baptized.

"What is baptized?" I asked.

"It's so you'll be protected by Jesus. People will sing for you and water will be blessed upon your head," Papa explained.

The baptism took place in a small Catholic Church, a basilica that was as beautiful as many of the old buildings in Milan were. Inside was cool and dark, lit only by candles. The priest wore a white robe with gold embroidery. His words were simple: "Holy Mary, Mother of God. Keep this child ever in your Grace. I now trace the sign of the cross on your forehead." And, with that, I was baptized.

This was my Italian self now. I saw it that way. One day we would be back to how it was, but for now, my name Ursula had a bigger meaning. It was no longer only the "little bear." I was now part of a bigger story, that of Saint Ursula who was martyrized (that means killed) in the fourth century. I understood this to be significant.

Mami was baptized too. Saint Mami.

As important as this felt, it never seemed enough. Day upon day, week after week, Papa still looked worried, often leaving the evening table to read the German newspaper. "What sort of nonsense is this?!" he shouted into the air one day after slamming the paper down on the arm of his chair. "Heim ins Reich!" It was a Nazi slogan, meaning, "Come home to the Fatherland," something the German government wanted all citizens living in territories not under German control to do. Brushing his hair back, a habit he'd picked up lately, he shook his head at Mami, saying only, "*Aber nein!*" This cannot be!

Then came a letter, all bright, marked with symbols and official stamps. "O Gott!" Mami screamed into her clenched fist when she read it. "Not this!"

Mami and Papa talked all night—or maybe only half the night and packed the other half. Because when I woke the next morning, all three of our trunks were sitting before the door.

"But Hans," Mami breathed, "Must this be?" To which Papa only shook his head and looked to the distance. "It will only be a short while, my beautiful. And when all this is over. . ."

That sentence was never completed. There was never a word that answered what was to be "when all this is over." But one thing was clear: We were going on another journey. A train, then a boat, and we were going in separate directions—Papa to the north, Mami and I south. But first to the government offices to post official papers.

Mami and Papa were to divorce.

It was the law of our country, the country to which Papa would be returning, alone. Why Mami and I couldn't come with him was never explained, but I understood it, like I understood to be *brav*. You just do what you're told. It was not a time for questions, and the answer was always the same, anyway. "It's safer."

At the train station, our trunks sat next to our feet. Papa took Mami in his arms. He kissed her on the mouth. He never did that in public. But this was Italy. Maybe it was all right to do here. Many things were all right to do here that weren't in Berlin, like singing in the street, like talking to strangers. I looked up at both their faces. Worry on his face; worry on hers. Then Papa turned away, taking two of the trunks and leaving the smaller one with us. Mami stood as if mystified. What had just happened? Her husband was walking away, his brown coat and brown hat blurring into the crowd. She was a woman alone now, no husband. Tomorrow was a silence that hung over us like a ghost.

Then, as if the thought had just occurred to her, Mami looked down at me and said, "We're going to visit Tante Hanni! And you have a new cousin now. A little girl, so small like Genevieve."

"Oh, Mami!" I exclaimed, trying to show my solidarity. We were going to get through this, whatever "this" was. "What's her name?"

"Hazel. It means something magical. In England, they believe the hazel tree gives you wisdom and even prophetic powers."

"Oo. I want to see Hazel!"

"Well, then, we will!" Mami appeared to have learned a lesson: Hoping didn't solve problems. Insisting did.

We boarded the train, just like the last one, and a two-hour ride was before us. Rocking side to side, I asked Mami all kinds of questions in Italian: What is that out there? "*Ponte.*" A bridge. "*Bambini.*" Children. And that? "*Soldato.*" A soldier.

We arrived at a city, Genoa, that smelled damp with much to see. Many people scurrying here and there, many going the same direction as we. Mami then told me our journey would take two weeks. I was frightened, but only a little. She said we'd have our own room. She called it a "berth." "And when we get to England, we'll be safe," she said.

I did not understand why she said "safe." Weren't we safe when Papa was with us? What does that mean now? "You'll see, my dear. We'll be with family and your baby cousin and you'll start school. And you can learn something new—English!"

I knew, then, that this would be a long, long holiday. But I was prepared this time. I'd already learned so much in Italy—all about food and how to say hello. I could certainly do that in England, and I was excited because I was going to start school.

People on the boat were either very friendly—chatting with me, asking about my pretty shoes and how I liked the sea—or they were very much not friendly and just walked by without even nodding "good morning." My Mami told me they were from other places with languages she didn't even know. I heard Italian, of course. But I heard German as well. A lot of German, and people who spoke German with accents. The help, the men who cared for the ship, spoke a language Mami told me was Greek, like the Gods. They looked like gods. Tanned faces and smooth black hair, always a kind word and sometimes a piece of candy for me. I liked them, mostly. Only one made remarks as he passed by. Once he spit. I knew it was on purpose, but he pretended it wasn't. Mami told me, "He thinks we're German."

"But we are, Mami."

"Yes, but he thinks we're a different kind of German. A kind he doesn't like."

"Well, I don't like him. And I don't want to be that other kind of German, either."

"Don't worry, my dear. You're not that kind of German."

"Is Papa that kind of German?"

"No. Papa is not that kind of German."

Mami woke early each morning to secure two deck chairs for us, then kept to herself and let me play as I liked. She wanted to enjoy the air; all I wanted was to play hopscotch. There were squares in the flooring that made perfect jumping boxes. Each time I'd try to jump farther, doubling up on the squares, and when I fell, I'd have to start all over. The Greek men laughed when they walked by, many times patting my head, saying, "*Buongiorno, bellissima,*" and I understood what they meant. They meant they liked my twirling dress. And I responded with "*Buongiorno*" and hopped on.

Mami chose the shadow side of the boat, the starboard side, because there was a better chance of finding two chairs together. I didn't mind not having a seat on the days she found only one. I would eat the lunch Mami made for me and sit on a blanket.

Out on the deck, out where the sea air blew forever in our face, were many moments filled with our own things to do. There was much to see, like seagulls and dolphins. Mami pointed to the shore sometimes to say, "Look! It's France!" or "Look, it's Spain!" And then we got to a place that she said was famous: the Strait of Gibraltar. There was land on both sides of the ship now. Once we passed through, it was open sea for another many days. This part made me rather seasick. Nothing but waves and rocking and a sky the same gray as the ship.

Slowly, slowly, one drizzly morning, we maneuvered into port. It was June already, a bit cool still, in 1939. The port was called Portsmouth, which I thought was quite appropriate. I learned already from Mami what a "mouth" was (*mund, bocca*), and "port"? Well, it was a port (*haven, porta*). That just made sense.

Sailors in uniforms and many waving people stood on shore. They let down the gangplank, and for the first time in weeks, we walked on solid ground. Time for Mami to worry again. I could see it in her face. I knew not to ask questions, although I had so many. We hurried along, pulling our trunk, me with Genevieve in my arm and a rucksack on my back that held my pencils, a notebook, and a handkerchief. And a special dress for baby Genevieve. I would put it on her tonight, I told myself. Once we'd settled and were sitting at dinner. I'd make sure she looked the part for the occasion. After all, we were in England!

We walked a short way. The chill in the air was letting up, but I kept my coat closed. Then we boarded another train. Mami said it was not going to be long. How much I hated hearing those words! They were never true, anyway. Yet, this did not take long, in comparison. We arrived in London two hours later, where we rode in a big black London cab to my Aunt Hanni and Onkel Werner's house.

What a flurry of excitement when they opened the door! Aunt Hanni picked Mami up and twirled her around. She stepped back and cradled her face with her hands, as if she couldn't believe who stood before her. "It's you. It's really you!"

"We're exhausted," is all Mami said. I didn't know what she was talking about. I wasn't exhausted. I wanted to meet Hazel. But no one asked me. And Hazel was down for her nap. Oh, how I wished the adults didn't always make the decisions for me!

Aunt Hanni kept giving Mami a gentle hug, shaking her a bit, and all the while exclaiming, "Ja, ja!" and "Come, we'll have tea. We should have a little champagne as well. Just to celebrate your safe arrival."

There was that word again: *safe*. What could she mean by that?

Tea was something the Englanders followed like it was a religion, Aunt Hanni told us. Every afternoon around 16:00, small squares of soft bread with butter, a banana, and shortbreads appeared on the parlor table, along with, of course, a freshly-brewed pot of tea.

As Tante Hanni laid out the cookies, the tea pot and cups, the sugar and clotted cream, she eyed us both, disbelief still in her eyes. "Do you know what the Nazis are up to now? Do you know? They're about to take Danzig! Danzig has been a free state since the time of the Teutonic Knights! Since King Arthur, or whoever, but I heard it on the BBC! Oh, Eleanor! You must listen to the BBC. The news they tell is so vastly different from what all the propaganda Göring used to put out. You should hear!"

And there was more and more talk about that and that and about "Hitler," and about "Churchill," but I wasn't interested. A church on a hill? What did that have to do with anything? I wanted to be excused. There were records and photos to look at, and books, and Hazel. I was sure she was soon to wake. . . and then I saw Mami do something as if in secret. She leaned forward and grabbed Aunt Hanni's hand. "Hanni," she said. "Have you heard anything? A letter, perhaps? Anything?"

Aunt Hanni shook her head, "No, my dear. I have not."

4

The Summer of '42

🌿 BOB

MILLBURY, 1942

I was eight and going into the third grade. That made my sister, Phyllis, fifteen and my two brothers somewhere in between. Phyllis was my favorite though. She was the one who showed me most of the things I needed to know in life, like how to aim a slingshot and tie my shoes. Phyllis walked me to the bus stop in the mornings and made sure I had my lunch. She even bought me a frappé (an icy-cold milkshake) at the drugstore lunch counter on occasion. Strawberry, my favorite. I heard some boys at school say she was a looker, and I kind of knew that. She had thick dark hair, full lips and cheeks, and she was tall, maybe five-seven or five-eight. For a girl, that was tall. Boys turned their gaze on her whenever she walked by.

It was August in the summer of '42 when our house became a flurry of excitement and anticipation. Ma had been packing things into crates: the special dishes, the gravy boat and soup tureen that only came out at Christmas and Thanksgiving. Areas I'd never noticed before, like the window ledges, were being cleaned. Shelves in the parlor turned empty, the books packed into boxes or off to Goodwill. More and more, the house became brighter, and sparse.

We were moving to a farm! I could not get over it. We were going to live with goats and chickens and dirt and apple trees, a real barn with a real hayloft. Everything I remembered from my grandparents' farm, only more. There were going to be woods, pastures and a creek to explore. Ma and Dad could not have been happier. Ma hummed to herself throughout the day. Dad kept chatting on and on about what he had done as a kid, even if no one was listening. Ma, I knew, just wanted out of the city, but Dad was "going home." The only one who wasn't in on the excitement was Phyllis. She wasn't happily packing up her things; she was moping. What this meant for her was losing the friends she had, some of them even had cars. Her prospects, in her mind, meant farm boys and little else. Where was the excitement in that? High school football games on Friday nights?

Then one evening at supper, the air felt somber. Dad looked to Ma, she to him, but there was no talking, only the silent clink of forks hitting the Melamine plates. What had happened? Are we not moving after all? And then I saw something I'd never seen before. Dad threw his hands to his face. His shoulders shuddered. It took me many minutes to realize he was weeping. Dad never cried. Only children cry. When they're hurt. But why Dad? Why now? Ma laid her hand on his arm. Even Baby Mary in her highchair, spoon in hand, stopped pulling at the diaper around her neck that served as a bib.

Then Ma announced something I could not comprehend: My Uncle Leo was dead. My Uncle Leo, who rumpled my hair and played horse with me on his back, me holding onto his collar, yelling, "Giddyup!" My Uncle Leo, who ice-skated with me and showed me how to shovel the pond in winter. That Uncle Leo? Yes, that Uncle Leo. He had been electrocuted, burned right in his seat.

We were reminded of the tragedy over and over. Neighbors came with hot dishes. The Worcester Telegram, delivered to the general store in large bundles tied with twine, showed his picture right smack on the front page: "Man Dies by Electrocution."

Uncle Leo had been driving a crane at the plant where he worked, moving airplane parts from one area to another. It was hard work with heavy equipment and heavy metal parts—airplane doors and siding, wings and propellers—machines that were needed for the war raging in Europe. One of the wheels drove up onto a palette causing the crane to tip just enough that the boom head struck an overhead wire, killing him instantly.

My eight-year-old brain could not fathom this. I had not lost anyone yet, and I didn't really know what dying meant; not yet. I only knew because my Ma told me. It meant I would never see him again. Ever. It was like dividing zero by zero. What I came up with was nothing. It just didn't make sense.

Our excitement for the move to the farm took on a whole new dimension after that. We were excited but we were all sad at the same time. Pa's youngest brother was gone. There was no changing that. But the day arrived—August 15, to be exact. That morning, Ma opened the door to the bedroom I shared with Paul and Sonny. The sudden bright light from the hallway woke me. What, so early? But I saw Phyllis standing by her side, already dressed, fists on her waist. A grin on her face that paled the hallway light as her eyes beamed right at me. Ma, all animated, announced, "Get yourselves up! We're going! Pepe will be here any minute. Pancakes are waiting; bacon is waiting. And so is the farm!"

Boy, we hurried something special that morning, rushing into our trousers, a T-shirt for me, and a quick comb through my hair with my fingers. This was a day that would change everything. We were going To The FARM!

Dad, Uncle Pete, and Pepe were out loading the rented trailer. All our boxes were already in it. They were now struggling with the "Black Stove," which truly was a black stove, black like molasses, with chrome trim all around. It had two compartments below: one for the wood fire, the other for the baking. Ma's washing machine came next. It was not quite as heavy. I could tell by the way the men talked about where to place it. "Easy now. Just slide it over thata way a smidge. . . There now, that's good!" It was a cylindrical tub with a handle at the side. Ma, or sometimes Phyllis, rocked that handle back and forth, churning the soapy water until the clothes looked decent and the water was gray. The jeans and sheets and socks then went, one at a time, through a set of attached rollers, squeezing out any left-over water. Then they were hung out on the line to dry.

The rented 24-foot truck was finally full of what was left of the furniture, bicycles, tools and crates and we were about to leave for the last time. I was allowed to ride up front inside the truck. I couldn't help thinking that it was my Uncle Leo's spot I was taking. Grandpa Ovid, who we called Pepe, was to drive our family sedan, the 1938 Chevy, taking Ma with my three-month-old baby sister Mary in her lap. Uncle Pete, my mother's brother, took the rest of the family in his car: Phyllis, Paul, Sonny, and Patricia, who was six by now. Uncle Pete was not happy about this arrangement, a car full of kids, all of them restless and none of them getting along much in the moment. Perhaps, there was just too much commotion for all of us over the weeks. The report was Uncle Pete kept shouting to be quiet, his right arm swinging back and forth behind the front seat as if that would make any difference. The ride was but five miles. But if you asked Uncle Pete about it, he'd have said, "Hours! Hours. Impossible hours!" All I knew was everyone tumbled out of that car in a real hurry.

We were here! I could swear the sun blazed brighter, the air smelled sweet and fresh. The adults were chiding each other and popping the lids off cold bottles of beer. Ma put a pot of spaghetti with meatballs on the stove, and we were about to have our first meal at 80 McCracken Road, Millbury Mass., picnic-style. As we all gathered around a blanket Phyllis had lain on the lawn under the shade of a broad willow tree, someone asked, "Where's Patricia?"

"Where's Patricia?" Ma repeated, looking to Uncle Pete.

"Well, I don't know where Patricia is," Uncle Pete said. "Didn't you have her?"

"I didn't have her. I had Mary. That was enough." Suddenly everyone looked around as bewilderment circled through us.

Oh My God!" came a chorus. "We left her!"

Luckily, Uncle Pete was, again, in a good mood and jumped into his Pontiac to make the drive down the winding dirt road. This time, it was without chirping children in the back seat. Six minutes later, he arrived at our now empty house in a cloud of dust only to find Patricia peacefully playing with her doll in her favorite spot behind the store, a nook she had created in the patch of grass where the root cellar door lay flush to the ground. She had just made "tea" and was serving it all around to a circle of stuffed animals, the ones Ma had told her to pack in a suitcase. Ironically, the suitcase made it to the farm; Patricia didn't. The adults sure had a good laugh about it, though, and Patricia was given an extra-large slice of Ma's famous homemade chocolate cake.

The afternoon sun cast a dusty gold color over fields that went on forever. I needed to go see. Passing the well, quickly tasting its fresh, cool water, I hurried along to the shed. It sat at the back of the barn, looking all mysterious and holding a certain draw. Something could be in there, I thought, something old, or new, I didn't care. As I got closer, I noticed the grass was moving unnaturally. There was a skittering in the dirt and a family of mice scurried into the daylight and back underneath the barn. Silence fell. I looked closer, then, because the grass started to move all over again. As I squatted and parted the blades, I saw the patterned back of a snake. It slithered away, and then I saw another. And another. I was struck with awe. So, there were snakes on this farm! This was a happy discovery.

Behind the barn, I found what could have been the reason for those snakes: a pile of grasshopper carcasses and fish bones. Someone must have been feeding them, I thought. I knew a little about snakes. I didn't think these snakes were anything to be afraid of, but Ma would never let me feed them or keep one for myself. This I knew for a fact, and so I moved on.

The cows were out in the pasture, grazing at this time of day. The two snorting pigs were in their pen, cooling in a slop of mud. On the far side of the barn was a small yard surrounded by chicken wire, and inside this yard were two ducks and a flock of chickens. Farther up? A whole eighteen acres of pasture and woods that needed to be explored, with grass and wildflowers up to my ears.

Life on the farm quickly took on a necessary routine. Mornings, at the first ray of sun, we went out for chores. Milk the cows, sweep the stalls, gather eggs, feed the chickens, feed the pigs and sheep. Since it was still summer and we didn't have school just yet, afternoons were for play. The older boys stuck to themselves most of the time, playing soldier with sticks they found on the property, and I often found myself alone. But I treasured those moments. There were giant oak trees that became my very own places to build my own forts and treehouses. There were birch trees with branches from which I could swing, pheasants to chase after, rabbits and squirrels, the pollywogs in the pond to stir sticks at.

Past the wild blueberry and raspberry bushes and on down a nearly invisible trail through the pasture, I discovered what would become my favorite spot. It was under a straight-up stone ledge whose shadow crept through a good part of the surrounding forest. I found mushrooms here. In the weeks to come, I picked them and brought them home to Ma. Black Trumpet and Turkey Tail; I knew which ones were edible and which weren't. My new life was a treasure to me I'll never forget.

It was early one morning, still with chores to do, that my brothers and I went into the barn, as we did every morning. First thing, Sonny flicked on the light: two lone bulbs that hung from the ceiling. We always visited our horse Maggie first and petted her muzzle. She was always ready and waiting. But on this morning, Maggie seemed different. Instead of nosing us to hurry with the oats, she turned her head, proudly showing us what she'd done in the night. There, right by her side, was a foal standing on wobbly legs. Eyes that looked too big for her head looked stunned to know such a beautiful thing as life existed.

It was hay season the month we arrived, and I got to see firsthand what real work was like on a farm. Dad borrowed a tractor and a mowing machine from the local co-op. Day in and day out, he was out in the fields for a good long time, cutting the tall stalks and loading them onto a trailer. When the trailer was full, he drove it back to the barn, where Maggie was hitched to a line with a large hook that had teeth. The hook, then, was hung out the loft door and dropped onto the wagon. With the help of Paul and Sonny, it was then clamped shut over a good pile of hay, maybe even a third of the trailerful, and then Maggie walked that rope, fed through a pulley, and lifted the pile right into the loft. I'd never seen this, certainly never in the city or even the corner store. This was so new, and so like Dad to know how to do something, like he'd been doing it his whole life.

"After school," Dad said one morning over a bowl of oatmeal with brown sugar, "we've some slaughtering to do. You boys can help." This was also new to me, but it would soon become a normal part of our lives. An animal lived with us, then it didn't. That's just how it was on the farm. We never named our animals, other than Maggie. It helped when it came time to put them out.

Dad shot the pig with a gun, right in the head. Dad told us it wouldn't feel anything. At any rate, it was dead, and that instant the pig became a "carcass." Hung by a rope from a pulley on the two-by-four rafters of the barn, the carcass was strung up by a leg. A barrel was brought over filled with hot water into which the carcass was lowered. This was to loosen the hair, which made it easier to shave off, and to peel the skin away. Dad then slipped in a long, curved knife to separate the meat from the bone. A table sat nearby, where Dad deftly cut up the carcass into what we'd be eating over the months to follow. The carcass was now "pork." What was not used as a roast or cutlet was later ground to make sausage, the meat stuffed into the intestines. Nothing went to waste. Once Dad had everything cut to his liking, the meat was thrown into a large tub and sprinkled heavily with salt. The roast we were going to have for Sunday dinner went into the icebox.

This icebox was a most useful appliance. Once a month a delivery man came around in a horse-drawn covered wagon; under the cover were huge chunks of ice wrapped in layers of straw to keep it from melting too badly. He'd ask Ma what she wanted and she'd look into his wagon to pick out the choicest piece. The delivery man then wrapped a leather apron over his back, and, with a large clamp, slung a three-foot by two-foot block of ice over his shoulder. He brought this into the house and it slid neatly into the bottom compartment of the icebox to keep our meat cold until the next time he came. It was Phyllis's job to dump the melted water from the lower tray of the icebox every so often throughout the day.

The other side of hard work, I was beginning to learn, was success, something we celebrated often when a roast was served and a prayer of thanks was given at the dinner table. We were, truly, thankful.

One evening after supper, I looked out the screen door and saw the night was simply too magnificent to leave behind. Fireflies filled the yard. The earth felt still warm from the day's sun. The smell of growing things was everywhere. I don't think I asked for permission. In our family it was assumed we knew our limits and we knew how to take care of ourselves, and when it was bedtime. All else was up to us. Often us kids went out after supper, to run, to play hide-and-seek, to check on Maggie. But this night was mine alone. I walked down the path past the clothesline, around and past the pigpen. I needed to do my own thinking. I lay down in the hidden grass and tucked my jacket under my head for a pillow. There I was, all to myself, as I stared up into the velvet sky with its millions and billions of stars. I made my eyes blurry and thought about what stories the stars might have to tell. Was there one just for me?

As I drifted into a state of wonder, my great-grandpapa Lewis came to mind, how he too was part of the land once, how he too knew animals. And it hit me like an epiphany: He looked at this very sky, these very stars. He saw exactly what I saw. I crooked my arm under my head and thought, I'm a very lucky young man.

5

This is War,
1938–1953

GERDA

A Journey

DECEMBER 18, 1938

Gerda brushed the second coat of dark lacquer onto her nails,
gazed at herself in the three-sided mirror, and reflected on the
fact she'd be twenty-nine on her next birthday. She shivered. So
much had happened in so little time, it made her dizzy. Was it
only a month since she boarded the steamship?

In the life before, she carried herself with monied elegance.
To see her was to think of jewels, of pearls. Invited one evening to
a club only the upper echelon of Berlin knew and frequented, in
the midst of dazzle and champagne, the man who would sweep
her off her feet approached her. His name was Harry Wachner.

A young businessman from Munich, he had recently arrived in Berlin seeking his next big venture. With a smile that sparkled as bright as the diamonds on his cufflinks, his outstretched hand and slight bow gestured his request for Gerda to dance, which they did until dawn. Two weeks later he asked for her hand in marriage, an offer she readily accepted.

Her Papa Sally would have none of it, though. "Why, he's a Münchner!" he objected. "What does he know of business in Berlin? Nothing! This is not who I raised my daughters to be!" With that, Sally had the last word.

Gerda and Harry decided to elope rather than try to persuade Sally otherwise. In the picturesque spa town of Bad Reichenhall in Berchtesgaden—ironically also the home of Hitler's "Eagle's Nest"—a rabbi friend of Harry's pronounced them man and wife.

Then Sally died. Herr Israel's grand Kaufhaus, while left in the hands of capable managers, soon ran into trouble. It was the times in Germany. 1937. A department store, now owned by his widowed wife and three daughters, a family of Jewish women no less, had little hope of surviving.

With the events a year later leading up to Kristallnacht, Gerda and her new husband realized, suddenly, that they needed to flee. Harry had heard of a place they could go that sounded impossibly magical. It was, however, 8,000 miles and a month-long seafaring journey away. Shanghai, China. It had started as a rumor in Vienna that Shanghai was welcoming Jews, no passports needed, and this rumor ran riot throughout Europe during the late months of 1938.

Shanghai had had a history of accepting immigrant Jews since the mid-1800s when a ragged group of 700 Sephardic Jews from Bagdad arrived as traders. Then, in 1917, several thousand more Jews, Ashkenazi this time, escaping the pogroms of the Russian Revolution, arrived. Now, with Nazi Germany's forced emigration, another 20,000 Jews would make the journey.

Roughly thirteen square miles of prime coastal land in Shanghai was known as the "Shanghai International Settlement," primarily governed by Britain, France, Portugal, Italy, and the United States. The police force, fire department and even a military reserve were maintained by this international committee. With the Japanese occupation of China, things did not change much. The International Settlement continued to rule, unimpeded, for several more years, as Japan didn't want foreign powers involved in their own war against China. Instead, Japan designated the Hongkew District of Shanghai to be the area where Jews were allowed (and required) to live, calling it the "Restricted Sector for Stateless Refugees."

The Jews made the best of this. The neighborhood became flush with bakeries, delicatessens, dance halls, and synagogues. Doctors and dentists, architects and lawyers set up shop. Jewish schools were erected. Musicians formed orchestras and played nightly in Jewish dance halls.

An Unusual Escape
NOVEMBER 16, 1938

It was a cold Wednesday and not yet dawn. It felt like it could snow. Gerda and Harry hurried from their home in Charlottenburg in such a rush that Gerda didn't even have time to kiss her beloved Amadeus and Marie Antoinette, two ridiculously cute shih tzus, goodbye. Her neighbor Edie promised to care for them. How long she was able to do so, Gerda would never know. When she returned, when the war was over, the neighborhood, including her home, was gone. No word from Edie ever again.

Gerda and Harry boarded a train at the Anhalter Bahnhof in Berlin, and fourteen hours later arrived in Genoa. Here Harry booked a first-class suite on a steamship. "What do we have to lose?" he laughed. "If we don't spend it, they'll just take it from us anyway."

Their berth was grand: plush parlor chairs and marble-topped tea tables. Elegant paintings covered the walls and crystal filled the mahogany shelves. They had a fully stocked bar. Nights they danced to a twelve-piece orchestra in a ballroom that accommodated a garden with real trees, the tunes always uplifting and full of promise. Within days, the terror of the Night of Broken Glass was soon forgotten.

We're Here

DECEMBER 19, 1938

"Wake up, darling," Gerda whispered. "We're here. Already I can hear the seagulls; already I can smell the wharf. . ."

Harry couldn't help but first tell her, excitedly, of his winnings the night before, how his luck kept coming, how their first night in Shanghai would be one fit for the queen that she truly was.

The ship pulled into port. Gerda's first impression was how the air shimmered with petrol fumes. On the docks she heard a melee of languages, only one of which she knew: Yiddish. Although their vehicle was chauffeured, it was a trishaw, not the Mercedes-Benz from times before. The apartment to which they were taken was small, a closet of a kitchen with a two-burner stove, next to which was a room with a pallet that served as their bed as well as their divan. But Harry remembered to carry his queen across the threshold, an image she would hold dearly in her memory for years to come.

Using her stenography skills, Gerda soon landed a job with a Jewish dentist. Harry, too, found work, but it was, in his words, "various." Sometimes gone, sometimes not, sometimes bringing home money, often not.

January rolled into February, and no heat anywhere. Not in the apartment, not in the shops. What Gerda began to do the nights when Harry wasn't home, was spend her time at Café Louis, where the entry sign read, "Each customer is God-sent." Here she was apt to find friendship and lively conversation with others who, like her, appreciated its nostalgic reminder of home.

1939 became 1940, Gerda continued her work and Harry continued his absence. He still flashed his charm with Gerda, still talked of big business once back in Germany, but the fatigue of life in China was etching its way across his face. His hands trembled now, his gaze was distant, and Gerda spent more and more time with her friends, Sara and Rosa, at the café.

It was a Friday afternoon in April, sweltering for so early in the season. Dr. Eisenstein sent Gerda home for Shabbat. She wasn't feeling well. But she didn't want to go to a home where she would sit alone and wait for a husband who, if he came at all, would reek of cigarettes and a stale shirt. It would be more than she could stomach, and she wanted the comfort of friends.

She made her way to Café Louis and ordered her usual *Kaffee mit Schlagobers*. "Sacher Torte for you, Madame? I believe there's a piece with your name on it!" the waiter winked as she seated herself alongside her two closest friends.

Gerda nodded yes, although the thought of it, the sweet, the cream that was mostly agar, the texture, made her stomach churn. She'd been feeling this now for some time, weeks, even.

"It's the meat here," Sara said. "They don't clean like they should. The knives—I've seen it—have flies on them. Even the Kosher butcher has become sloppy."

Rosa disagreed. "No, no. You cannot eat anything from the market, let alone the fruit. They have insects here we aren't used to, and they land on everything."

But it was April. There were no insects. And Gerda had not eaten meat in nearly a month. It sickened her to think of it. It wasn't that. It was everything else. As she sat staring at this thing, this Sacher Torte she normally loved, Rosa shook her head. "Gerda, you don't look well."

Gerda felt the tears rising in the back of her throat.

"Oh, Gerda," Rosa said quietly.

"I know," said Gerda.

"When did you find out?"

"Only a couple of weeks ago."

"A couple of weeks? That's not so bad. Are you sure you're not just, you know, nervous? With all these changes, living in this strange land, nowhere to go but our own little *Shtetl*. And in China!?"

"Look at me, Rosa, Sara! I've been sick. Every afternoon, at night. I run from my desk to the toilet. I haven't the nerve to tell Dr. Eisenstein. He's been so good to me. And Harry? Harry, if I tell him, he'll only talk more of the grand business he'll run when we're home in Berlin. He won't care if it's a boy or if it's a girl. Why, I can't imagine him even holding a baby. *Schmutzige* diapers and vomit on his collar? He'd rather collect rotten cabbage rinds off the streets!"

"Gerda, you'll be all right," Sara said, and handed her some sour plums she kept in her purse. "These'll help. And, Gerda?"

"Yes," Gerda said, tears dripping from her chin.

"You'll be all right."

DECEMBER 12, 1938

Lloyd's of London quotes odds are 32 to 1 against Britain being involved in war before the end of 1939.

SEPTEMBER 1, 1939

Germany invades Poland.

SEPTEMBER 1, 1939

Operation Pied Piper evacuates 1.5 million Britons, including 800,000 children, to the countryside in England. Over 2,000 school buildings are requisitioned for the war use.

SEPTEMBER 3, 1939

Britain declares war on Germany.

URSULA

Not What I Expected

SEPTEMBER 7, 1940

London certainly was a stark contrast to my two previous cities. What I remember of Berlin was the happiness: Papa arriving home, often middle of the day with a sweet for me in his pocket, playing with my dolls on the veranda, Klara calling me in for tea, summer breezes and losing myself in the garden. Milan, too, was sunny nearly always, and there, Mami did her best to remember to sing.

Perhaps I believed that happiness would return once we stepped off the boat in Portsmouth, once we'd arrived in London, once Mami had found an apartment. But that happiness never came. People hurried here, with heads bent. Every room felt damp, and dark. I missed my Papa. But this was something I didn't want Mami to know. I could see she was trying hard to make our life good, so I talked about it only to Genevieve.

Our apartment on Ossulton Way was much like our home in Milan. The rooms were large and the doors tall, but the kitchen was small: a ceramic sink under a narrow, smudgy window, a small gas stove, a shelf for our cups and plates and a cramped table just large enough for two. We had little furniture and there was a perpetual feeling of anxiousness. Mami's face showed it, and when we visited Tante Hanni and Onkel Werner, I saw the same. I didn't know why, and there was always chatter going on in whispered voices as if someone was not supposed to hear. But who was that someone? We didn't have servants anymore. I just didn't understand it.

Then came the big news. It was everywhere. In the streets, and Mami talking to Tante Hanni quite excitedly on the telephone in a worried sort of way. It had happened. Britain and France declared war on Germany. I had just turned five.

Christmas was not the joyous time I remembered from before. There were no candles here, no *Lebkuchen*, and at Tante Hanni and Onkel Werner's, there was no tree. Mami said it was because of the blackout. No lights were to be seen from the outside, so things were kept dark. I felt sorry for Hazel that she wasn't able to know what Christmas was really like. But it was the times.

The New Year brought about a change everyone had been anticipating: rationing. Meat, sugar, cheese, butter and eggs could only be bought using a ration card. But that was not the worst of it. Clothing, soap, fuel, and paper simply ran out. And all this alongside the dreary weather.

It was September. I was to start school. I had turned six a month earlier, and I was excited to no end. That first morning, the sky was a luminous blue. Mami held my hand as we walked through Hampstead Garden Suburb up to my new school. I had to admit,

I was also a little afraid. How would my accent be taken? Would I understand everything? The words and sentences in my new language were coming to me quickly, as if they were already inside me just waiting to come out. But still.

My teachers were kind, taking me to the side sometimes to help me with my figures, which did not always come easy. For example, seven plus four, or eight plus five.

One week went by, and it was Saturday. Mummy (I quickly learned the new pronunciation) decided we should spend the day on Hampstead Heath. It was not far from our home, and the weather was pleasant. We packed some cucumber sandwiches and cream crackers and strolled along Highgate Pond. We talked about everything, saying it all in English. Our destination was Parliament Hill, a "hefty" climb, as Mummy put it. But we managed.

At the top, after we found a stone bench to sit upon, after we helped ourselves to our picnic, Mummy pointed out the sites. "Look, there's St. Paul's Cathedral. And there, look there!" she said. "The famous Tower of Big Ben!" Her excitement excited me too. We looked and exclaimed about so many more places, including where, if we could see it, we lived.

It was so lovely to sit with just her, the quiet, nothing but the chirping of crickets. But it was time to go, and so we made our way back to the Underground.

We had just come home, my coat still on, and Mummy was beginning to prepare tea, when there was the most terrible loud noise I had ever heard in my life, so loud, I screamed. BOOM! BOOM! BOOM! I held my ears shut and ran to Mummy. Then it came again. BOOM, BOOM! My mouth was as wide open as it could go, as I screamed as loud as I could, all with my eyes shut.

"Come, fast, child! Fast, fast!" Mummy shouted and pushed me under the stairway, ducking quickly behind. For two hours we stayed there, Mummy stroking my hair, whispering, "It will pass, darling. It will pass. . ." while the explosions continued.

For two hours we held each other, and our bodies shook. I tried hard not to whimper, but I was very frightened.

Then, all went still. Mummy and I stayed where we were, under the stairs, and held each other all night.

On that day, September 7, 1940, 348 German bombers and 617 German fighter planes flew over London, dropping incendiaries that destroyed all of London's docks as well as countless homes, factories and shops. We had no way of knowing how long, or how often this would happen, but these attacks would continue for fifty-six more days, bombs falling on each of those days but one. Mummy and I made up a bed of cushions from the sofa and blankets and pillows from our beds under the stairwell landing. Here we slept every night, leaving room, of course, for Genevieve on my pillow.

On September 22, a German parachute bomb landed right on our street, Ossulton Way. A baby that had not learned to walk yet, was dead, and there was a house not far from ours that now had the whole front missing, the parlor with sofa and table in broad view from the street, a bathtub hanging in mid-air.

Rubble and broken paving stones became a common thing, houses with blown-out windows. I became used to the whir of planes overhead, and barrage balloons were a common sight, drifting, large and ominous, around the city.

DECEMBER 29, 1940

This time we ran to the Underground for shelter as all our neighbors did. I was shocked to see people, whole families, putting up house. Rows of mattresses placed between the rails. Boxes with teacups on them. A burner for the kettle. Here and there were small Christmas trees with decorations. A man joked, "The stable in Bethlehem was a shelter too, wasn't it?"

We crouched as everyone crouched. And then it came: the

whistling, the deafening, terrifying thuds, the ack-ack, again and again. Terrifying moments in which everyone held their heads beneath blankets, even inside suitcases, anything to feel, for the moment, protected.

Then the wait for the all-clear.

This time, this dreadful time, the all-clear seemed to have forgotten us. When it finally did sound, when we finally emerged from the Hampstead Underground (the deepest station in London, thought to be the safest), we were met with a heavy wind blowing debris in every direction. Looking toward London proper, the sky was ablaze in red, and there was a strong smell of things burning.

The neighborhood warden escorted us home. Jovial as he was trying to be, I could tell he too was shaken. "Appears we outwitted the Jerries once again, eh, Mrs. Krehn? Come, come away from the walls, now, lass, will ye?" he panted. With every passing person, he had the same to say. And everyone felt so very thankful for him. "Of course, of course, Mr. Garrison. . ." I heard over and over.

In time we would learn over 100,000 incendiaries had been dropped by the Germans, causing a firestorm with winds so strong, they pulled small animals, prams and rooftops up into a tornado-like inferno. Hundreds of people were killed, 13,200 homes, 31 guild halls and 19 churches as well as the entire publishing district of London were destroyed. Five million books went up in flames. Even the beloved St. Paul's Cathedral had been hit.

Mummy had had enough. The next day we moved to Wokingham, 37 miles west of London. It was quieter here. We could still hear the bombs, but they felt less real. No longer did we sleep under the stairs, and I could finally focus on my studies. I was determined to be a girl like the other girls in my school, one who spoke clear English. German, I gathered from looks the students gave me, and looks their mothers threw my way when they walked their girls home, was not a favored language, and Berlin was certainly not a prideful place to be from.

MAY 11, 1941

After eight months of bombings, the London Blitz comes to an end. In all, 43,000 people were killed, 8,000 of whom were children. Two million homes were damaged or destroyed; 60 percent of them were in London.

Slowly life began to feel manageable. I was excelling in school, even my math grades were 8s. Mummy let me study dance. She loved the arts, too, and was all too happy that I had a chance at it. It was mostly ballet, but a fascinating form that was taught on the side was country step-dancing, like drumming with your feet.

One Sunday Mummy suggested we visit Tante Hanni, Onkel Werner and Hazel in London. "The streets are safe again and, anyway, the sun has popped out!" Mummy said. "We can stop for some crumpets to bring and oh, wouldn't it be so lovely to see Oma Martha again?" Mummy seemed particularly exuberant, and I was always happy to do something when it was the two of us together. Tante Hanni and Onkel Werner, although right in London, had managed to avoid the bombings. At least their house was spared when many around them weren't.

It was at the table with our tea and the crumpets we'd brought from the market, I saw Mummy do something she'd done before. She leaned in and spoke softly. "Have you any news?" Again, I saw the lines of worry across her face. "Do you suppose he's, well, dead, or something?"

Hanni didn't say, "No, I've heard nothing." She simply moved her head back and forth real slow. Then she grabbed Mummy's hand and gently shook it. The look on her face was strong.

"Eleanor. I really have not heard anything. Keep your faith.

But my dear, there is so much more, and my heart sinks to tell you this. It's what I've gleaned from news from the BBC reports. I worry about your mother-in-law. She has the name, you know. Mendelsohn. They say the Germans have put all Jews into camps. We cannot know for sure, but they won't distinguish a German from a Jew, mark my word. They took her!"

"Oh, Hanni! This is why I prefer to listen only to news about the defeats, the battles the Allies are winning. What's happening in the country I'll never call home again, is just too gruesome, too fantastical to understand."

The rest of our teatime took on a black mood. Clinking teaspoons made more noise than voices did. I suppose it was the silence that follows when you know something evil had been spoken.

Her name was Luisa Krehn when she was my Papa's Mami, but when her husband, Mr. Krehn, died, Luisa was remarried, this time to a man named Mendelsohn. This was the first I knew of the origins of my middle name, Luisa. I had always wondered at the spelling, Luisa, with an "a," not an "e," Luise. But now that I learned it was my Papa's Mami, my ears perked up.

We would not learn what happened to my Oma Luisa until after the war ended. But, true, she'd been taken from her home by the SS a day after they took her husband. The reason was "Suspicion of housing Jews." "Housing," in her case, was living with a husband who was Jewish. Much later, when I was already an adult, I saw a German poster, dated October 15, 1941:

> *Verordnungsblatt für das* Generalgouvernement, p. 595, . . . Jews who have left their designated residential area will be punished with death. . . the same penalty applies to anyone who knowingly provides refuge to such Jews. This includes providing a night's lodging, food, and any other aid, such as transporting them in vehicles of any sort. . . .

It wasn't until then, as an adult, that it hit me. Surely this was what happened to Frau Luisa Mendelsohn, my Oma. Sachsenhausen, situated in Oranienburg, 37 miles south of Berlin, was the concentration camp thousands of Berliners had been sent to. In 1940, when Oma arrived, the work detail was "shoe-running." Prisoners carrying full packs were required to run around a parade ground along a path made up of varying surfaces. The purpose was to test the durability of different shoe soles. Here, she stomped, back and forth, day in, day out, through the blazing summers and icy winters, for the duration of her internment.

Sachsenhausen was liberated by the Allies on April 22, 1945. Luisa had been released sometime before that, but she was sent out on foot. She had to walk the 37-plus miles back to her home, perhaps wearing the very shoes she'd been testing. She could consider herself lucky, though. She was at least alive when tens of thousands of her co-detainees had been taken away for extermination.

Luisa was not the same after that. She was old already when they took her. She was very old when she returned. But she was my Oma, and I could not help but feel a little grateful for the resistance she played in this war, as difficult as it was. What she suffered gave my name a meaning I vowed to cherish from then on.

DECEMBER 7, 1941

Japanese bombers attack Pearl Harbor.

DECEMBER 8, 1941

The United States declares war on Japan.

GERDA
Calamity

The more the baby grew inside her, the more Gerda found refuge at Café Louis, where the first thing she wanted was a glass of iced plum juice, sweetened with cane sugar. She was convinced it alone helped with the sickness. Chinese lore proclaimed it also helped against the "heatiness" of the unbearable humidity brought on by the daily rains. Sitting off in her favorite corner, she noticed, on several occasions, a man with tanned, bulging biceps under the tightly rolled sleeves of a work shirt.

"Erich Bayer. Aus Bayern!" He was chuckling at his own joke when he introduced himself and bowed graciously before this beautiful woman. He'd been a banking accountant in his life before but now worked the docks unloading military provisions for the Japanese.

Erich was a jovial man who wasn't fazed in the least that he'd been reduced to manual labor after a prestigious position at Deutsche Bank. He rather relished it. A man devoted to fitness and a life outdoors, his new work suited him, and this impressed Gerda.

Time passed and they fell into long talks over everything and nothing—the heat, the flies, the cramped living conditions. Never did they mention that nothing was known of family back home.

"How is it?" she asked one day. "Working with the China men? Do you get along?"

"Ach!" Erich smiled. "We have a bit of fun! You know the 'Japanese Occupation' around here is a joke. They don't have enough soldiers in all of Japan to 'occupy' every city in China. Gian—we call him Johan—taught us Germans the words to a song they sing, and we mimic the refrain right along whenever the Japs strut by. 'Arise! We refuse to be slaves! With our flesh and blood, let's build our new great wall!' The Japanese? They think we're idiots."

Gerda was more than amused and even invigorated by Erich's stories. They made her feel less despaired, less forsaken, less pregnant.

Then, one glorious winter day, the midwife came to Harry and Gerda's apartment to deliver their little girl. It was December 23, 1940. Her name would be Steffi.

There were weeks at a time now when Gerda would find herself in the home, caring for darling Steffi, alone. Harry, it was no secret, had become an avid gambler, and his days away from home lengthened to weeks at a time, with no more than a quick "hello. . . goodbye" when he did return. With the dwindling money, the lack of heat and drafty hallways, Gerda became more and more despondent, and she spent more and more time talking with Erich, who loved to play with a one-year-old teaching her to blow kisses. There were times that Erich, Gerda and Steffi ventured out onto the docks, even, Gerda and Erich holding hands.

It was rumored that Harry had a new woman. Wei Li was a name that was mentioned, an eighteen-year-old waitress in the gambling and opium house, aptly named "Hollywood," and if it was Wei Li, it can be surmised that she finally put her foot down: "It's either me, or her. No more, 'my wife, my wife!' Decide or go!"

And in her way, Gerda said the same: Leave.

The process was straightforward and simple. A Rabbi witnessed the signing of the divorce papers which took less than an hour. Harry shook Gerda's hand and together they walked out the swinging doors into a crisp autumn afternoon, the sky so white it hurt the eye.

Where Harry went after the divorce is anyone's guess. Perhaps he moved in with Wei Li, although the love affair lasted only until Harry left China. Likely, her father didn't take a liking to this flamboyant *Gweilo*. "And yet," he would have equivocated, "This is war."

Gerda was a conscientious worker and never missed a day at the dental office. But now as a mother, alone, things were difficult. Steffi was a toddler with a two-year-old will of her own. However, Dr. Eisenstein, a kind man, arranged for his wife and a neighbor friend to help with the childcare, and the days became routine. As did Gerda's visits with Erich, who now often showed up for dinner, and coffee on Sunday mornings.

"Steffi needs a Papa," Erich said to Gerda on one of these mornings.

Gerda stared at him. Then she jumped and threw her hands to her mouth.

"Are you saying what I think you're saying?"

"Exactly." Erich got down on his knee. "Will you be my wife?"

No further words needed uttering. Gerda was in love, Erich was in love, and even in these mad years of uncertainty, weddings were the glue that kept the community strong.

"It's like the letter 'A'," Erich beamed at her with adoration.

"You've a way with words, Erich! What on earth do you mean?"

"It's like one leg leans against the other. It's like that, that we need each other, or we'd fall flat."

"Plus, it's the letter that comes first." Gerda laughed.

DECEMBER 11, 1941

The United States declares war on Germany.

URSULA

Learning

I was now seven and could understand some things. I understood that our enemy was the Nazis, which was different than if we had said "Germans." For me, still, the German people were who I knew—my friends Frieda and Heidi. They probably wanted this war no more than we did here in London. The Nazis, my teachers explained, were the bad people in Germany. Their leader was Adolf Hitler. And our leader, a good person, was Winston Churchill. I learned about the *Hakenkreuz*, of the Nazi flag that was copied from India. My teacher said it was backward, and "backward symbolizes evil." She was from India; she knew. We also learned about the Third Reich, that Hitler wanted his Empire to be as great as that of the Greeks and greater than the Holy Roman Empire had ever been.

"But who will win?" I asked often, mostly of my Mummy. I didn't understand why it had to be bombs. Couldn't they just decide on a winner and be done? But no. The problem was Hitler wanted to take England away from us, and for that even I was incensed.

Mummy assured me it would go in our favor in the end.

"Why?" I asked. "How do you know?"

"How I know, darling, is that the Americans are now with us. The Americans have war machines and soldiers and money. We need to be patient. But good wins out in the end, always." This is something I explained to Genevieve. I was meticulous in my details, because I didn't want to forget any of them myself.

Mummy got a promotion, and we moved back to Ossulton Way in London. She would now work for a company that built machines for the war effort. I was proud: She was, in her way, working for what was right. With her raise in pay, she was able to enroll me in the Marie Auxiliatrice Catholic School for Girls. It was a strict school, Mummy explained, but it would help me become the best I could be.

My teachers were nuns with names like Sister Gregory and Sister Placid. Then there was Sister Eustace. She was a short nun with stubby fingers whose nails were thick and arced. On her lip were traces of a black mustache. Her mouth held small teeth with spaces between them, their color more gray than white. She let me know, in no uncertain terms, it was imperative I lose my accent. It was never again to be "Ja," even though I rarely ever said it anymore. Only sometimes. "Now," she corrected me, "it's to be 'Yes.' 'Yes, Sir. Yes, Ma'am.' "

Maybe it was something I shouldn't have done. I was nine already, in a school where I wore a navy blazer with gold braid on the pocket and a pleated skirt. But I did it anyway; I sneaked Genevieve into school, hidden in my schoolbag. I took her out only at the end of the day so I could tell her about what I'd learned. It was really good, because it helped me remember.

Sister Eustace was famous for her ruler. She liked to snap it against her hand as she walked between our desks. Sometimes she whacked it against a student, right on the back of the hand in which she held her pen. I didn't ever want her to do that to me. I silently named her "Sister Obtuseness." At least it was a good English word to know.

One day my fountain pen needed ink, something I should have taken care of before class, and this was math, my worst subject! I hurriedly rummaged through my schoolbag, hoping I wouldn't disturb the others. Sister Eustace, though, noticed immediately and had something to say about it.

"Ursula!" She barked, like it was a curse.

"Yes!" I stood and locked my knees. I wanted her to know I

didn't mean any harm. But she didn't let up. She walked—no, marched—over and asked to see inside my bag.

"You don't have chewing gum, do you?"

It was something I'd seen soldiers do in the streets, chew gum. I'd asked Mummy what it was; their jaws never seemed to stop. But I'd never tried it before. "No, Sister Eustace. I have no chewing gum." Then she leaned down and reached into my bag for who-knows-what. Out popped Genevieve's blonde curls.

"What. Have. We. Here?!" Sister Eustace exclaimed, yanking my beloved doll out by her head, not even straightening her dress when it flipped up. "What is this?"

"It's my doll, Sister Eustace. She's named Genevieve, Sister."

"This is a Käthe Kruse doll! Where did you get it? It's German! Do you hear that? German!" She spit out the words as if they tasted bad and strutted to her desk, plopping Genevieve into her bottom drawer. "You may sit in the back, Miss Krehn. You should feel grateful you're allowed to stay in the class at all. Shame on you!"

I cried all night long. When I drifted off to sleep, I woke myself up to cry some more. Genevieve now had no one. And I was responsible for that.

Then it was over. The next morning at breakfast, alone without my doll, I vowed to be *"brav."* I would miss her, but I would never cry again.

JANUARY 20, 1942

The "final solution" is determined. It does not go unnoticed
that the villa on the Wannsee where the Nazis decide
all Jews are to be exterminated is quite near the villa the
family had when Ursula's Papa was still with them.

GERDA

End Times

DECEMBER 9, 1941

Heinrich Himmler ordered all the names of anti-Nazis, in other words, Jews, in Shanghai to be handed to the Germans. The Japanese governor, curious about this request, asked Rabbi Kalish, "Why do the Germans hate you so much?"

Knowing the fate of his community hung perilously on his response, he answered, "They hate us because we're Orientals." The governor recognized the covert message, and a slight smile broke onto his face. His decision was to not acquiesce to the German demands, and the names were never released.

Approximately 18,000 Jews were, however, forced to leave their relative freedom and move into a ghetto surrounded by barbed wire and shared with an already crowded population of 100,000 Chinese and 8,000 other refugees. Rooms fashioned from former barracks housed anywhere from six to fifty people. These rooms, no wider than a narrow hallway, were lined with bunks: the uppers for storage, the lowers for sleeping, entire families to a pallet. Clothes were strung from ropes that ran along the ceiling. Cooking was done, year-round, on the rooftop; communal toilets, no more than a board with cutouts, were on the ground floor.

APRIL 30, 1945

Adolf Hitler is dead by suicide.

6

The American Side of Things

BOB

DECEMBER 11, 1941

The United States declares war on Germany.

NOVEMBER 8, 1942

Termed "Operation Torch," the United States launches its first campaign in the European theater with surprise attacks in Morocco, Algeria, and Tunisia.

I Knew Some Things

1942-1952

There was no news more exciting. One day Japan, three days later, Germany. The talk was everywhere. At the drugstore, Ma talked with the druggist. At dinner it was Ma telling Dad what she'd learned. After dinner, we heard radio broadcasts by Edward Murrow, his distinctive voice addressing our nation each night with, "This. . . is Vienna," or "This. . . is London." His breathy pause after "This" added such suspense that the stories seemed to unfold right as he spoke.

I was seven, and I was captivated. I listened to adult conversations; I quizzed my parents. Even though I was only beginning to read, I scoured newspapers and, at the movies, I intently watched the newsreels, wonders upon wonders. I followed the bombings in London, troop movements, casualty reports. I learned the types of aircraft, artillery, tanks, jeeps, warships, submarines. There were the military officers, admirals, generals, first sergeants and buck privates. Doughboys, swabbies, leathernecks.

Even here, in the hinterlands of Massachusetts, the threat of war became real. Air raid warning test sirens sounded at random times, so loud you'd have to stop and wait for the wailing to pass. The Sheriff stopped by our house more than once to make sure we understood to keep the lights out and shades pulled. There could be a time when those sirens would mean something.

George and Phillip both lived a mile and a half from our farm. That's rural living: Three miles away was considered close; one-and-a-half was "spittin' distance." We were best friends and were together nearly every day. There were woods to explore, rivers, ponds and railroad tracks to hike, but even with us, the war held its presence. We'd find sticks and suddenly become soldiers. No one wanted to be the German, of course, so we drew straws. Somehow it came to be me most often. Those straws were rigged, I was sure.

We loved everything about sports: reading about them, arguing about the scores. We traded baseball cards and listened intently when the World Series was broadcast on the radio. Not only did we follow the big players, we all wanted to be big players. And we played every game we knew: football, basketball, and, of course, the big one—baseball. Ted Williams, arguably the greatest hitter ever (no player has ever matched his .406 batting average), was—no surprise—my personal hero. I aimed to follow in his footsteps—bat like him, run like him. I might have been a little guy, but I was a tough one when it came to sports. All of five-foot tall, weighing ninety-nine pounds, I was on shortstop for baseball and the running back for our football team, and even made a great point guard when it came to basketball.

George took the lead in putting our name on the map. Through his church, he managed to scrounge together teams for all three sports: eleven men for football, nine for baseball and five for basketball.

Gus was the coach for our basketball team and had an in with a manager at Norton Abrasives, a company that manufac-tured sandpaper, sanding wheels, and just about everything to do with grinders and saws. And Norton had a regulation-size basketball court where they let us play on Saturday nights. We got to be so popular—the buzz of the town—that the Worcester Telegram and Gazette posted our box scores each Sunday in the weekend edition.

Then there was the Blackstone River that called to us regu-larly. It ran a half mile behind George's backyard, where its flow was already so wide it was impossible to ford. This predicament brought about a whole new big idea. We were going to build a raft. This river simply begged us to. There were beaver and Indian stake-outs, deer and rabbits, forts to build.

With our rudimentary construction skills—George had helped erect his Pa's barn, and I knew some things about fixing chicken coops and fences—we fabricated a very fine raft: thick birch branches tied with twine and a long thin elm limb for a push pole with which we worked to traverse the water, Huck Finn-style. On our first outing we tipped the raft, all three of us having to swim to shore. But that did not deter us. We just needed to fortify our vessel, which we did. No sooner had we tied off our raft on the other side, than the battle between the good guys and the bad ones began in this unknown territory of the north bank.

Sometimes it was Cowboys and Indians, more often Germans and Army Men, but at times it was Huck and Tom. "Y'all can be Tom and Huck all you want," Phillip shouted out. "But I'm Jim! There ya have it! And I'm not 'bout to call y'all 'Massa'!"

Life on the farm went on as farm life does. I turned eight, then nine, and sports and horsing around took second place as I was now old enough to contribute to the family's needs. Besides my farm chores—milking the cows, mucking out the stalls, listening for the hen's cluck that announced she'd laid an egg—it was time to earn money.

One of our neighbors was a 2½-mile walk down a dusty road shaded only by the occasional dogwood tree. His name was Sam Johnson, a Danish immigrant who spoke with a heavy accent. Sam and his wife were skilled horticulturists and, along with their son Arne, they ran an efficient, orderly greenhouse business.

Arne had thick hair that poked into the air like a scrub brush, his wheat-colored eyebrows and lashes were nearly invisible against his burnished skin. Arne was in charge of the outdoor garden: watermelon, tomatoes, cauliflower, artichokes, broccoli. What I learned from him that I never knew was that asparagus also came in white. In the early spring, Arne took the seedlings Sam had started in the greenhouse and planted them in mounded rows outdoors. Then he covered the stalks with dirt to keep the chlorophyll from forming. Each morning before dawn Arne went out to cover any shoot that had sprung up overnight. This meticulous process produced a tender white asparagus stem by June that garnered a premium price at delicatessen as far away as Boston. The Johnson Farm name came to be famous throughout the surrounding metro areas, especially in the European delis.

Sam worked inside the greenhouse, and this is where I was put to work. We grew flowers here and boxes of vegetables seeds to be transplanted after the last frost. My world was perfumed by hydrangeas, marigolds, pansies, and roses. I watered and dead-headed. I helped customers choose box plants and load them into their pickups. Memorial Day was especially busy, when families came for seedlings but also cut flowers for the sons and brothers fighting the wars abroad. With every name they uttered, sometimes tearfully, I reflected on my own life and wondered how I would one day fit in. I was only nine. But I knew some things.

Money, at the end of the week, went to Ma to pay bills, but she always remembered a small allowance, enough, at least, for a ten-cent movie or a Coke at the drugstore. All this is not to say I didn't feel sorry for myself those long days, straw hat on my head, counting out change for my customers while George and Phillip were laying out bases and arguing who was going to ump. More than a little sorry for myself.

But it helped me reflect on the big things.

Every evening, the family perched around the radio to hear what had occurred in Europe and in the Pacific the previous day. Edward Murrow, Lowell Thomas, and Ernie Pyle became household names with their captivating human-interest stories of the "infantry man at war." After Ernie Pyle was killed on the frontline by enemy fire, President Truman said of him, "No man in this war has so well told the story of the American fighting man as American fighting men wanted it told. He deserves the gratitude of all his countrymen."

Of course, we didn't know he'd be killed, or even how dangerous his job was. We just loved hearing him speak. The way the stories went, like the soldiers were personal friends, made me feel I was right in the heat of it, and something inside me said, *I want that*. I didn't even know what "that" was. It was the excitement, perhaps, the not knowing how things would end, but, mostly, it was the hope for a better world that had me want to belong. I will never forget his haunting sign-off: "Good night, and good luck."

The summer of '43. The war was nearly two years old. Nevertheless, the news kept me spellbound. I became keenly interested in geography. And strategy. And I had to circle back to a question that plagued me from the start: Why was our first attack against Germany fought in Africa? The answer didn't come immediately. My Ma and Dad couldn't say, the newspapers didn't say, and radio reports covered what was current: battles in Italy and France.

When battles started to be announced as Allied victories, I began to surmise—that first move was brilliant! Germany had to take much-needed troops from Russia to send to Africa, as well as the countries in Africa where we fought French protectorates—nowhere near loyal to the Vichy government of the Axis. And, with these assured victories in Morocco and Algeria, the US Congress was easily convinced that entering the war in Europe was a good idea. Someone was thinking!

On June 6, 1944, the United States, Britain and Canada launched the largest sea-born invasion in history. Although the Germans had anticipated a western shore attack, our misleading radio communications fooled them into believing it was going to take place in Calais, the closest point to England, which made sense. But Normandy, 400 kilometers to the south? It was a risky plan and thousands of Allied (as well as German) troops would die, but General Eisenhower, now in command of all Allied forces, determined it had to be here and now. Or never.

June 5 had been the original D-Day—"D" being a military term used when the exact date is a secret. But the weather that day was windy with heavy cloud cover and choppy waters. Postponing the attack by one day could still work, but any longer, the plan would have to be aborted. Eisenhower took his chances.

Once again, General Patton faced off against Germany's General Rommel. The battle lasted two months, three weeks, and three days, and has come to define the ultimate Allied Victory over the Nazis.

The German General Rommel, who'd been implicated in the July 20 (1944) assassination attempt on Hitler's life, was given a choice: commit suicide or face a trial that would result in disgrace and execution, anyway. Rommel chose to take a cyanide capsule on October 14, 1944. He was honored with a state funeral. The reported cause of death was "strafing of his vehicle while in Normandy."

SEPTEMBER 2, 1945

> Germany signs an unconditional surrender
> agreement with the Allies.

Hitler thought Americans didn't have the will to win. Boy, was he wrong! To add to the giddiness, the radio replayed excerpts from Churchill's outstanding speeches.

> We shall fight on the seas and oceans. . . we shall
> fight on the beaches, we shall fight on the landing
> grounds, we shall fight in the fields and in the
> streets. . .

Every city in the US held parades in the streets. Jubilation! The war was over! Soldiers were coming home! Then just a child, even I wanted to jump in the air with my arms raised and shout, "Victory!"

We began to see military surplus items for sale everywhere—gas masks, canvas duffle bags, canteens, combat belts, boots, cargo pants, helmets—and George's dad found the crème de la crème, an Army-surplus jeep, the neatest thing since hotdogs came on a stick. It was a dark army green with cutouts instead of doors and a canvas top; three-on-the-floor. Not to make a pun, but that jeep was a gas.

"Army! Navy! Air Force! Marines!" We shouted and thought nothing of sneaking the keys from George's Pa's hiding spot behind his Bible in the rolltop desk. There were empty dirt roads to master, a sand pit and mounds of gravel to attack, water-filled gullies and enormous ruts to traverse, thickets, a copse of trees. We pretended to be Rommel (defeated) and Monte (the winner), driving around the dunes of the Sahara, all the while thinking about those brave men who died on the beaches of Normandy. Who drove this jeep once? Did he survive? To put it out of mind, we shouted, "Hooah!" and carried on. After all, the Allies won and that's all that mattered anymore.

When the day was done and the fields turned golden, we replaced the keys and went home for dinner as if it was just another day. When it became winter, we drove that "green machine" out onto the ice of any one of the frozen ponds around us: Breierly, and many without names. Here we drove as fast as we could go, then pulled on the hand brake, whopping donuts all across the pearly winter land.

In 1947 the most amazing news came. The St. Louis Cardinals were holding tryouts for their minor league. I wanted to play ball so bad I could taste it. Would I take a day off from the greenhouse? In a New York second! My all of five-foot-eight and cocky as they come, I managed to make the first round. I was delirious. My head full of baseball dreams—I'll go to the pros! "Bobbie Langway! Another Grand Slam!"

What I didn't know was how badly I played as well. When the second round was called—and I was up against some of the country's best from high schools as far off as Florida and Alabama—I saw what I didn't even know yet was possible.

In short, that ended that career.

It was on one of those baseball nights, coming home sweaty and hair full of weeds that an ominous presence hovered over our sitting room. I didn't know what it was, but a deadness filled the air and the whole family was looking at Phyllis: Ma, Dad, Sonny, Paul, and Patricia. And Phyllis? A puddle of tears.

The Sheriff had accused her of murder.

Two months earlier, she had met someone who, for me, was the loveliest man alive. A Marine. A man with a strong smile and a wit to match. He was at dinner nearly every evening from the time they met. True. Phyllis attracted the lot of them. Men loved her with her thick lashes and tawny skin. Cat calls, quick touches when she walked by. So, when Eddie appeared, I thought nothing of it. But I could see he was in love. He pulled the chair for her, he gently touched her hair, he nuzzled her neck and made her smile.

I looked up to him something fierce. "Son?" he said to me out on the front porch one evening. "Not sure what you think of your future. But if it were me, I'd consider the military." I nodded and thanked him. He genuinely seemed to care about me. He then told me it had made a "man" out of him and he would forever be thankful for that. He said it with a twinkle in his eye that I knew was special, just for me.

It was on a Saturday afternoon. Eddie and Phyllis had gone out to Slaughterhouse Pond, the local swimming hole. The women spread chicken sandwiches and Cokes around; the men in their swim trunks climbed the surrounding cliffs to assess their immediate futures. They were, of course, all about to jump.

Perhaps it was to impress her. No one knew, but Eddie hiked to the highest point of the craggy wall, Phyllis in tow. There he stood, right foot ahead of the left, rocking back and forth. The other fellows goaded him, and there was Phyllis, saying something at his side. Something either to encourage him or discourage him. Only the wind knew. And then he dove, head between his outstretched arms, legs flopping loudly against the water's surface as his body submerged. Everyone waited for Eddie to pop up and raise his arms in a self-congratulatory handshake, as all the other guys had done. Eddie didn't pop up, though, not for what seemed like more than a minute. And then he did, face gushing blood from a gash on his forehead.

Things progressed rapidly after that. Friends rushed out to help him into a waiting ambulance and off to the hospital emergency room, Phyllis, in shock, up front with the driver. Eddie was wheeled directly into surgery. It was clear something bad had happened.

To get straight to the worst, Eddie died on the operating table.

Over the days that followed, law enforcement started to investigate, and Phyllis was a prime suspect in what could be construed as murder. What did she say before he jumped? And did he really jump? Or was she close enough to have. . . pushed him maybe? The ordeal, the questioning, the Sheriff showing up unannounced, traumatized her to such a degree, she didn't trust herself to leave the house. She was soon exonerated, but not without an emotional scar that took years to overcome. It took falling in love with a new man, someone who believed in her, and professed to care for her for the rest of his life.

His name was Mel.

In 1949 Phyllis and Mel married. Mel was an enterprising young man who offered me what amounted to a "real job." I was fifteen by now and earning substantial money seemed like a good thing. Mel happened to know the owner of a corrugated box manufacturer, who promised me a managerial position. In hindsight that was probably too big a job to offer a fifteen-year-old, because I didn't last long. My job was handling a rather complicated machine that, because of the responsibility, also paid more money, and my supervisor did not like the idea from the start. The nepotism rang too loud for him. After two weeks, I begged to be let go. Phyllis understood and Mel acquiesced, but not without some hesitation, because he had bigger plans in mind: He wanted to open his own box company and saw me as a potential partner. But that idea did not appeal to me.

Nothing was really appealing to me, and this became troubling.

An Air Force veteran named Dan Donovan opened an ice cream shop in Millbury soon after the war. Known as "Uncle Dan," he set out to make "Millbury's Finest Ice Cream," as the sign posted between his wide striped awnings advertised, awnings he was seen unwinding each morning and rolling back up at night. With a lunch counter, a few booths upholstered in silver vinyl and a flashy jukebox, Donovan's became the local hangout.

It was now 1952; George, Phillip and I were three of sixty graduates at Millbury High School. With a long summer ahead of us, we sat at Donovan's most afternoons with a Coke or a coffee and fed the jukebox with nickels. Sometimes when the mood hit us, we'd pull a girl in to dance when a singer like Percy Faith came on. But mostly our time was about us boys. These sessions came to feel important as we were getting on in life. Decisions needed to be made. What to do now that high school was over? Certainly, college was out of the question. There was no money for that and in 1952, only 5 percent of Millbury's high school graduates even thought about attending higher education. There were jobs, most certainly, but we weren't all that interested.

For Phillip and George, the decision came easy: both joined the Navy. My story was more complicated. I knew I didn't want to be my dad, a painter and wallpaper man, and the idea of a factory with corrugated boxes was not speaking to me either. Often, I walked home with my head spinning and no solution in sight.

Funny how things can change when you put your mind to it, though. On one of those starry nights, my mind all abuzz, I tried to talk some sense into myself: *George and Phillip are going into the Navy. What's so wrong with that?* The Navy doesn't appeal to me. *But what about college?* There's no money. *Oh, but, but!* What'd you say? *Didn't you hear Phillip talk about when he gets out in four years the VA will fund his tuition? And pay for books?* Okay. . . *What's four years?* Dunno. *You're eighteen; you'll be twenty-two in four years. Think about it! College! No one in your family has ever dreamed this big!*

That was that. Before the summer was out, my bag was packed. I kissed Ma on both cheeks and gently closed the farmhouse door behind me. I walked the half mile to the bus stop and did not look back. I was on my way to Air Force enlistment training.

7

In Paris

URSULA

On May 8, 1945, Germany surrendered unconditionally. It would be hard to exaggerate the euphoria we felt. The air itself was filled with song. Church bells rang, bicycles swerved through the streets, automobiles honked and people waved at each other to "Carry On," but with a brand new meaning. A youthful energy coursed through our bloodstreams. It was a time to rebuild. From the station conductor to the postman to the milk store, the baker, even the nuns at school had a new glow to their cheeks. And so, the news that Mummy had a new job did not surprise me in the least.

We were living in Manchester by now, where I attended the 400-year-old Loreto Catholic School for Girls. A change was not unanticipated, but what surprised me was that the job she accepted wasn't anywhere near where we lived. She was going to Germany, alone. It was for a rather prestigious job, too: interpreting at the war trials in Nuremberg. For the interim, I was now to attend Our Lady of Sion Convent in Bayswater and become, for the first time, a boarder. I was eleven.

JACQUE GUERIN
Conflicted

Germany's invasion of France in 1940 lasted six weeks, after which the Nazis occupied the country. In order to control the French people, a new Vichy government sympathetic to Nazi ideals was put into place under whose authority Jews were deported to German camps and France became a police state. It was no secret that the population of France was an unwilling captive and nearly from the start, a clandestine organization, calling themselves the French Underground, burgeoned.

Jacque Guerin, a captain in the French Army before France capitulated, decided, rather than be taken prisoner by the Germans, to defect and join in this resistance. In his later accounts, he listed that he and his band of rebels had bombed trains, blown up munition dumps, flooded canals, cut train lines, aided Allied pilots caught behind Axis lines and "did anything to sabotage the Nazis."

His hideout in the Pyrenees was raided in 1943, after which he was sent to an *Offlag* (Officer's camp) in Germany, where he was interned with other *maquis,* as they were called. At first, he was merely questioned, but the Nazis felt he knew more than he was letting on. Hoping to uncover the Underground's system of communications and their hideouts, Jacque was moved to a solitary cell, from which he was dragged all hours of the day and night for interrogation. The cross-examination quickly turned to abuse. He was slapped, punched, kicked in the stomach, often sent back to his cell bloody and barely able to breathe, only to have it repeated the following day.

What changed, he didn't know, but one day, he was deposited in a "holding camp" that was surrounded by a chain-link fence topped with rolls of barbed wire. All the "holdees" were French, bodies bared to the elements with no water or food. Residents of the village jeered at them. Sometimes they threw bread over the fence just to watch them grovel. Once a rotten hog carcass was thrown in, something so fetid, that, hungry as he was, Jacque couldn't bring himself to fall onto it like his fellow prisoners, vying for just one morsel of the stinking flesh. By the time the Allies liberated his camp, as many as half of the prisoners were dead, and of those still living, many had severe illnesses including gangrene from festering wounds.

Jacque had seen the worst, and had fought fiercely. As a witness to the Nazi invasion and the inhumane treatment in the camps, Jacque was invited to give testimony at the trials in Nuremberg. Presiding over the trials were British, French, US, and Russian delegates. These trials got off to a rough start, often becoming stalemated as the parties simply couldn't understand one another, particularly the Russians, who had few interpreters that spoke both German and at least one language other than Russian.

This is where Eleanor's work came highly appreciated. Because of her impressive resumé, her mastery of foreign languages, and the fact that French was her first "second language," she was paired with a number of key French witnesses. When it came to Jacque Guerin, the file was thick: French Resistance. Escaped. Captured. Informant.

Germany's Nuremberg represented a symbol of the Nazi heyday and, for that very reason, was chosen as the location for these trials. Although by the end of the war three-quarters of Nuremberg lay in ruin (with 90 percent of the old town nothing but rubble), Hotel Deutscher Hof remained miraculously undamaged. It was this hotel that was used to house those attending the trial. Which was no mistake. Jacque's apartment was only a few rooms away from the notorious number 105, once Hitler's private suite.

Eleanor entered his suite, a two-room apartment that appeared to have just received its room service of coffee, bread and jam. He wasn't exactly handsome, but he was striking in his black turtle-neck, piercing gray eyes and Brilliantined hair that reflected the sunlight filtering in through the louvred blinds.

"It says here, you're thirty years old. You're quite young to have experienced all you did," she said in perfect Parisian French. "Was it. . . twenty-five when you enlisted?"

"That's correct, Madame. My father died in the first war. Unnecessarily. I couldn't let that happen to my mother, lose her husband and then her country, twice."

Their interviews continued for many weeks and with each revelation, Eleanor became more incredulous. "They marched children into the streets, alone? Their mothers thrown into separate lorries? What did the police do? The ones there to protect them?"

"Oh, believe me. They weren't there to protect anyone. They were following orders, which came from Berlin. Make no mistake. The Vichy government had nothing but their own interests at heart. Their money, their possessions. Do you think they cared about snot-nosed rascals from the streets of our hamlets? There was a larger order at work. Make no mistake."

To Eleanor's disbelief, Jacque meticulously described the atrocities, the unprovoked deaths, the strange demeanors of his captors. His bravery, of course. He was, she detected, rather full of himself. But why not? He'd killed, by his estimation, sixty-seven Germans. And saved? He didn't know, but there were old women in headscarves and young boys in short trousers also engaged in the secret Underground. How many saved? Several hundred? He really didn't know.

Eleanor began to bring pastries to their talks, which often

lasted well into the evening. He asked about her life, and she said she had a daughter. "I do too," he said, becoming solemn. "She's not with me anymore. Her mother didn't approve of my choices. Her family was quite wealthy, you know."

"Do you know where she is?"

"Sadly, the answer's no. I believe she'll look for me one day. I'm her father, after all. But. . . the war. . ."

To this, Eleanor looked to her lap and repeated the same. "Yes. . . the war. . ."

As she rose to leave, as Jacque held her coat, there was a gentle brush of fingers that they both noticed. He said, "Au revoir, Madame."

"Au revoir," she replied.

URSULA

A Fracas

I didn't exactly dislike him, but I did notice his eyes narrowed when he looked in my direction. But Mummy was so happy, so lighthearted, she sparkled. It was 1948. I'd been in the convent now for three years. I'd been a studious girl, and had many friends. I had nothing against my circumstances. In fact, I felt quite lucky. I was in the most prestigious school in Britain, supported by a mother who earned the kind of income most fathers only ever dreamt of.

Mummy was reserved, but not submissive toward him, this Frenchman, Jacque. What she wanted was for me to say, Yes. How could I not? She was my mother. But I didn't like this man.

The wedding was small. Me in a dress I had embroidered myself with pink flowers. Mummy looked stunning, as always, in a gray fitted suit, a bouquet of red roses at her waist. Jacque? Colorless.

The ceremony was traditional, ending with the liturgical

crucifix that Jacque and Mummy held while the priest blessed it, saying, "You've found your cross, a cross to be loved, to be carried, a cross to be cherished."

Why Aunt Hanni didn't come, or Uncle Werner, or Hazel, I'll never know. Perhaps they knew what I felt: He's too French for us.

The three of us moved into an apartment in Bayswater, London, a stylish neighborhood, very near Kensington Garden where I spent many an afternoon, whiling away the hours until teatime. At home, Mummy was aflutter, making meals and ironing the bedsheets—anything to make us feel like family. We were to stay in London, I'd continue my schooling at the convent, and Jacque would find a job. That was the plan.

It didn't go well. Not even two weeks, and two things were already different. One: I was to go to summer camp, in the Alps. And two: Jacque announced, "There's nothing for me in England."

The prospect of summer camp away from the oppressive situation at home and away from rainy London, was an exciting one, and I agreed readily. "You'll learn to speak French," Mummy said, "so you can converse with your stepfather, who. . ." Here, she put her hand to her face as if she had a terrible toothache. "He's been through so much, you know, beatings, forced marches through the snow, starvation. Perhaps with you at camp and the two of us here, things will settle in a bit."

I didn't protest. Perhaps she was right.

Then, I was on a train to Verbier. I'd not been to a camp before and the outdoor activities certainly tired me out. There were daily French lessons, art classes, dance classes, good food (as we were always hungry), and sing-alongs around a campfire at night.

The language lessons came rather easy, but they were also tedious. Why, I asked myself, did I need to learn yet another language after I'd already mastered English, and Italian? My resistance, I believe, had everything to do with *him*. Why was it up to me to learn to communicate? Why not him? And then I decided, *I'll just get really good at it, and he'll have nothing to say.*

Then something happened that erased my attitude altogether. I befriended my bunk-mate, Claude-Elie. A delicate girl with a soft voice, luscious blonde hair and porcelain skin. Claude-Elie let me know she was here because of her father. "He doesn't like me," she explained, in slow deliberate words: *"Il ne m'aiment pas."*

The passion with which she said it grabbed my heart. It was something I'd been wanting to say for a long time about Jacque: *Il ne m'aiment pas.* We became fast friends and made a pact: I'd speak only English and she'd reply only in French. After two weeks, it seemed to have worked. We both felt more confident in our new languages and I felt I might even like this new man in my life.

Which brings me to the second change. While I was away, Jacque and Mummy decided we should move to Paris, a complete shock to me, but it was what he wanted.

It was early June now; the rosebushes were just beginning to bud when, with our trunks packed, furniture sold or given away, we boarded the boat-train at Victoria Station and awoke the next morning at Gare du Nord in Paris.

Not only were the roses in full bloom, the chestnut trees were brilliantly decked in red flowering clusters. Jacque, through his aunt, a countess no less, acquired for us a modest, but sumptuous, apartment on Boulevard Raspail in the 14th arrondissement, a neighborhood that reminded me of where we once lived so long ago, Charlottenburg, with its chichi boutiques and cafés. Within a three-block radius of our home were all the important shops we needed, each selling its own wares: wine, milk, pastries, the fishmonger and the butcher. It became a daily event, walking to each store, becoming comfortable with the language: "*Qu'est-ce qui est frais aujourd'hui, madame?*" What's fresh today, m'am?

Jacque took a job at the Metro. His managerial position was to file reports for the delays that occurred at any one of the many stops the trains made each day. I couldn't understand how this job meant anything. And, anyway, how silly he looked, walking out the door in his tightly buttoned jacket and brown pillbox hat. I was not about to let it bother me, though. Paris was simply too interesting a city to let someone like the *petite grenouille*, (which is what I secretly called him), cloud my day. It was a term Claude-Elie taught me: not exactly flattering to call a Frenchman "little frog," but it kept me amused.

Mummy, who I now called Maman, had just finished unpacking the last box, setting the last teacup on the shelf and laying out our worn tablecloth, when Jacque, home for his *sieste*, announced, "Things need to change."

With firm lips and darting eyes, he continued. "It's not working. A fourteen-year-old in these cramped quarters will never let us, Eleanor, dear"—with these last words softening his voice, his gaze rested on her—"get to know each other."

What are you saying, Jacque?" Maman stiffened.

"I'm saying, *she* must go. We need time together, and a girl her age. . . why, she takes up space, your time. Time I want with you!"

Maman's eyes fluttered briefly; she inhaled. "But, Jacque. . ."

"I just want what we had in Nuremberg, our long talks, we held hands, our moments of silence. . ."

I was intrigued more than anything. I knew Maman would not desert me. But I also knew how hard she wanted to please her new husband, younger by eight years.

"I've made arrangements I believe are agreeable to all parties." Jacque smacked his fist into the palm of his hand. "The Countess."

"The Countess?" Maman said.

"She has a daughter, alone and lonely in that cavernous château. She'd be thrilled to have a playmate—or I should say, 'young woman'—with whom she can spend her days."

"But, Jacque!" Maman looked to me, distressed. "Must we? I mean. . ."

"It's the best. For all. And look, my love, we're only a few kilometers away. Surely Ursula will thrive."

There was more he said, Maman protesting (but not that hard). I could see she was resigned to the proposition, and, to be honest, the idea titillated me. A château? A friend? A family and no Jacque?

The countess's château was indeed a castle. I had my own maid, my own driver, my own wing, breakfast in bed—although a luxury I couldn't get used to. It wasn't served before 11:00! I asked the cooks if I couldn't eat, instead, with them, at 7:00. It was a bit of fun then—early awake, a quick soft-boiled egg, a cup of milk-coffee, then off to Versailles' gardens only a short walk away, where I would sit on a bench with my diary and write. It helped me sort out all that had happened and most of all, it helped me in my uncertainty.

Monique proved to be an enjoyable, if bashful, friend. Mornings, after our croissants and bowls of half milk, half coffee (she began to join me in the kitchen with the cooks), we strolled through the château's park-like grounds. Monique told me the names of plants, what an *urn* was in French, what a *folly* was. We talked about art and books and Monique told me she knew something secret: how to get into Versailles through a side entrance.

She told me about the French kings, how Louis XIV invited the public into his chambers each morning to watch him dress, how the royals were beheaded during the revolution, and people came to watch even that. About how King Louis pranced along the "hall of mirrors" just to watch himself walk.

"How ghastly!" I said.

"Yes," she remarked. "But you must understand, he and his mother were terrified he'd be assassinated. Like, he HAD to be enamored with himself." With stories like this, Monique made Paris come alive for me, what with all that history and art.

Monique, too, loved to dance, and her mother, the countess, enrolled us in private dance classes. "Not to let your Papa know!" she warned me. "He's sure to disapprove."

And oh my! The dance classes! I was introduced to something I'd never seen before. It was called "tap." It was much like the step-dancing I'd been learning at the convent, only different, faster with more shuffle-ball changes and real "stomps," some of it to music I'd only recently started hearing: jazz.

The countess one day came home with a new pair of shoes for me. Black patent leather with taps and each with a fat red ribbon to tie it shut. Oh, how I loved those shoes! Monique and I practiced then, day after day, in her "playroom," the room she had had as a child, still filled with a dollhouse the size of an icebox, a rocking horse and shelves full of dolls and stuffed animals, books and board games. "Not to tell the Papa, yes?" the countess winked when she passed us, sweaty and giggling, coming out of Monique's room. My new Papa? The very thought of him, the apartment with the rank kitchen, his white shirt with the yellowed armpits, made me shudder.

It was August. My birthday came and went. No one noticed. Not even Maman phoned. I felt blue, thinking, "must be how the rich do it." And then it dawned on me—I didn't know Monique's birthday either. I vowed to find out, and what I discovered was she would also turn fifteen in only a month, something we promised to celebrate together.

It didn't come to pass. I was summoned home. Maman discovered there was a baby growing inside her, and she begged Jacque to allow me to return. She needed the help. Surely Jacque couldn't deny her this?

Steely-faced, I arrived, determined not to upset my "Papa," determined, too, to be a grown-up daughter to Maman, helping where I could. One evening I was preparing a platter of cheeses and cutting a baguette, when I noticed something red inside the rubbish bin among the wilted daisies I'd thrown out just that morning. I looked closer. That was *my* red ribbon, off *my* shoe! And when I reached in, there was the other ribbon, both were still attached. . . to my tap shoes!

"What on Earth?!" I shouted. *Mert!* Who? What?

Just then my Papa stepped in, arms folded across his chest, eyebrows lifted, ready to scold. For shouting. For being here. For anything.

"You threw them away, did you?" I screamed, pointing at the rubbish bin. "Tell me you did that!"

"I did that!" he bellowed, his voice egregiously lacking remorse. "No self-respecting girl dances to *that* sort of music!"

"What sort of music might *that* be?" I shot back. I was fuming, and yet, I knew, unless *he* returned the shoes, unless *he* apologized, his word would be law.

And that's exactly how it went.

"There's no arguing, Ursula, so stop your belly-aching. You're old enough to understand that kind of dancing only leads to trouble. And, that. . . is my last word!" He kicked the refuse can (with a scruffy-toed shoe, no less!) and slammed the door behind him.

I threw my dish towel on the table and huffed off to bed. I knew, then, I hated him. No dinner for me, and I didn't give a damn. He could eat those shoes for all I cared. I was going to provide for myself from now on. I spent the night dictating, in my head, all the things I'd say to him next time we talked.

And then, on December 29, all was forgiven. An angel arrived in our home, Anne-Marie. I couldn't get over how tiny her perfect little fingers were, how perfectly her lips formed an "o" as her infant eyes regarded the light, her maman, me.

I helped Maman with feeding, diapering and bathing the little cherub. I called her "Mimi" because she was too adorable for such a long, hyphenated name as Anne-Marie. On sunny days, I wrapped her in blankets, set her in her pram and took her for strolls through le Jardin du Luxembourg. Mimi pointed, giggling, at the flowers along the promenades, and I loved the mysteries of the Medici fountain.

At home, I stayed out of Jacque's vision. I was loathe to call this small frog, "Papa" ever again. Perhaps that added to his frustration, but I didn't care. Let him be Maman's problem; he was not mine.

Another baby came along eighteen months later. Again, the tiny fingers and perfect mouth, but this little fellow was a feisty one. His name was Yves, a perfectly lovely name for the handsome child he grew to be. And precocious! By the time he could talk, he knew every car. Standing at the balcony overlooking the traffic, he'd point and shout, "Peugeot! Citroën! Renault!" excitedly stomping his plump feet.

These two little people brought me all the joy I needed. Happiness was such a fragile thing, I realized, on short supply sometimes, like it was on rations. But if I kept what I cherished close to me, my happiness could only be thwarted if I let it. So, I didn't let it.

Then the bomb hit. Jacque announced once again he was unhappy with his station in life. What with his standing as Captain in the French Army and his service to his country in the Resistance, he should have risen to a post more becoming of his stature. Running daily reports from his office to the Métro's headquarters was not all that flattering. He deserved more. In his opinion, at least. And he'd found the perfect solution that he announced at dinner that night.

"I'm going to work for an American company!" Jacque, at the head of the table, glowed as he waited for us to give full attention before he continued.

"That's wonderful, Jacque! When. . . where?" Maman was enthusiastic and I, too, wondered if it would help his mood.

"It's for Coca-Cola!" He pulled out a flyer from his attaché case that, apparently, he'd nabbed at his interview. *From Cape to Cairo: The Sun Never Sets on Coca-Cola!* it said above a drawing of a buxomy blonde holding a bottle of the dark elixir to her cheek. "See what you get with a Coke?"

"I'm going to head the new offices in Casablanca—that's in northern Africa—" he said, disparagingly.

"Oh my!" is all that Maman could utter. She didn't know where to begin. What about school for the little ones? And, our apartment? Let alone. . . what about Ursula?

Nothing was decided that night, but the questions loomed.

The next morning, she was fussing with Yves' breakfast cereal, stirring to cool it off. I put my arms around her waist and whispered in her ear. "Maman. I'll do anything if it'll make your life easier."

It wasn't entirely unselfish of me to offer a separation. In fact, I took comfort in the idea. What I saw before me was the opportunity to be away from him. "You're worried about me, no, Maman? Don't be. I know I need to stay, at the very least to finish school at Alliance Française. Go to Morocco. You'll find your place. And. . . I'll be with you soon." I promised to keep up my grades, to eat well, to make sure the apartment stayed tidy.

Maman spoke to the landlady later that day, asking if we could keep the apartment, that her daughter (who is very neat and a great helper in the home) would make sure it was well-kept.

Things moved forward in such a hurry, I didn't have time

to think what it would be like without my little sister and brother around. Let alone, the quiet that came with everyone gone. There were tears and hugs, but mostly consolation—"Maman! I promise to write. Once a week, I'll write!"

In my silence, once the door closed behind them and I looked around at the apartment that would now be mine alone, I went to work putting my life to order. The first thing I did was phone Claude-Elie, my friend from French Camp. I rarely had a chance to be with friends, given all my responsibilities. But now? Now, I was free! I knew she lived in Paris. But I didn't know she lived only a block away. "Oh, Ursula! Come to my house, quick! I'll make some coffee. I just bought some *pain au chocolat*. It's still warm!"

Oh, I ran to her building and when we saw each other at the door, we hugged and danced about. It had been several years, but we recognized each other instantly. "You're as beautiful as ever, Claude-Elie!"

"But I was to say the same to you, *ma chére!*" she giggled. "Come, sit! We have so much to talk about. Ursula. . . you say you have your own apartment now?"

"Yes, yes. But I must stay vigilant. The landlady is quite a nosy one. But we'll have so much time to spend together, Claude-Elie!"

Hour upon hour we talked and played our records, trying to do the funny steps to the dances we weren't yet familiar with, the "jitterbug," for instance. Claude-Elie, I discovered, was unhappy at home. Sometimes her cheeks were red. I couldn't tell if they were because she'd been slapped or if she'd been crying. She never said. But she did say her Papa was iron-fisted. I wasn't sure how to take that, and I never asked. He seemed to have forgotten she was only a girl. He shouted at her for the littlest things. She was to have his dinner ready, for example, but never did she do it right. She should keep her coat buttoned up. "Each time I come home, day or night, he grills me on where I've been. Who with? A boy? I say, 'No, Papa. I'm with Ursula,' but he doesn't believe me."

He soon married his deceased wife's best friend, a widow who'd cared for her while she was dying. Madame Caillou was no better, though, constantly yelling, making Claude-Elie responsible for everything that went wrong.

"My home life was not much better, Claude-Elie. He never once commended me when I received good marks, or a teacher praised me for an essay I'd written. But boy oh boy, come home with a pair of tap shoes! The house nearly exploded for the fuss that created. He threw them in the rubbish bin! Brand-new—and I'm sure expensive—dance shoes!"

To make up for our loneliness and to keep Claude-Elie away from her dismal home, we began to explore the city. We took boat rides in the Bois de Boulogne, shopped on the Champs-Élysées and visited the Louvre. We watched American films at the cinema. *A Place in the Sun* had just come out. "That man! I dream of him!" Claude-Elie confessed one day about Montgomery Clift.

"Well, you'd better hope he's dreaming of you, too, and not Elizabeth Taylor!" I said, and we both doubled over in laughter.

Laughing. That was our favorite thing to do, in particular while making fun of American tourists. "Money, money, money, money. . ." we'd sing-song, and already we cracked up. One day on the Champs-Élysées, we followed a pair of well-dressed American women who were window-shopping Gucci and Chanel when I heard one of them remark at how ungrateful the French people were, "after all we've done for them."

This last piece irked me and I couldn't help but translate to Claude-Elie that, in her opinion, the French were so poorly off that they needed American money just to pay for heat in winter. One of the women turned around and scolded me, saying in perfect French, "Young girls with such big ears should wear extra-large earmuffs." We found it funny, the women found it funny, and we had a good time repeating the episode with varying versions as we sat at Café de Flore later that day with our *chocolat chaud*, creamy and thick with a pitcher of Chantilly cream on the side.

Café de Flore and Café les Deaux Magots in the 6th ar-rondissement became our "spots," where the likes of Ernest Hemmingway and Gertrude Stein, not to mention Jean-Paul Sartre and Simone de Beauvoir, once sat. It was where we now, too, sat in the midst of cigar smoke and blue absinthe, finding it fascinating how the men became chattier with each glass, some-times inviting us to join. We, of course, had better things to do.

We soon discovered the nightlife in the Latin Quarter. We learned about *les Caves* and frequented them often, and often for the lower-priced Sunday matinees. Les Caves were literally caves, underground, where wine was once kept. Cheap to rent, musicians loved the atmosphere. Two-tops lined the narrow sides, while at the far end on a dimly-lit stage a singer with a saxophon-ist or pianist belted out the most extraordinary American music.

Louis Armstrong and Sidney Bechet played one night. I had *never* heard anything like it! People stomped their feet. A woman jumped on her table and started to clap and move her hips. People danced the jitterbug.

Then one night, Dizzy Gillespie was to play at the Théâtre des Champs-Élysées. We desperately wanted to see him. He was the jazzman of all jazzmen, the one put the razz into jazz, no question.

Here we were, two school-age girls, with no man escorting us. The maître d' simply ignored us. Up ahead, there was a group of Irish boys, about our age, who noticed our distress. "*Vous deux! Venez ici! Vous deux!*" "You two," they called out. "Come up here!" Finally, the doorman acquiesced, pushed us ahead and said, "*Passez les bons temps!*" Have a good time! The boys found us chairs; we ordered Oranginas, and the night was on.

I had no idea who Harold Nicholas was. But one night in Les Caves I watched him dance his magic. A slow swoosh, a fast tap-tap. . . I locked eyes with him as we sat right up in front. Then he brushed his toe, real slow, in my direction and hopped up on top of a table and flipped his hat.

I dissolved into tears.

He was wearing a red bow tie. It reminded me of what I had dreamed I could do one day, dance just like him. What he did for me that night was show me that sometimes life doesn't turn out like you expected. I wanted to jump on the stage and thank him, because I realized too, that if you look hard enough, there's a hidden gem waiting for you inside. I can't say exactly how that was communicated. But I will forever be grateful to him for that moment.

And to the Irish boys.

8

Air Traffic

 BOB

A Higher Purpose

From the moment I hopped on the train at Worcester Union Station, my thoughts were in the clouds. Me, on my own, and about to see the world. I stared out the window the entire hour to Springfield, where I was going for "enlistment indoctrination." I wasn't even sure what that was, but I'll bet I floated six inches off the ground when I walked into that office.

First the physical and inoculations—if I was going to die, let it not be from tetanus or malaria. Then there was the aptitude test, called the AFSC or Air Force Specialty Code. I knew some things about farming, gardening, and manufacturing boxes. What I didn't know was that I was also good at electronics, commanding officer assistance, radar operations, control tower operations, and pilot communications. I couldn't understand how they determined all these important-sounding jobs. What it would be in the end remained a mystery for some time yet. Meanwhile, I was issued military clothing, boots, dog tags and an M-1 30-caliber rifle. No real ammunition allowed, but target shooting was on the agenda.

I'd hunted rabbits and birds all my life so I was feeling pretty sure of myself. This time, though, I was on my belly, with my rifle out in front and eighty rounds to shoot at a man-sized target. My instructor was a patient man. He showed me how to breathe, how not to jerk when I pulled the trigger, how to adjust the sights. If I could hit the target thirty-five times, he said, I'd get a ribbon. Needless to say, my hot-shot-self didn't pull through. But then, no one's did.

We were taught to march in step; we bivouacked overnight and learned all the military acronyms, like AWOL and its severe punishment; we learned how to address an officer and each other, how to keep our shoes sparkling and our uniforms pressed. We drove in a jeep simulator to test our response times. Given I'd already had my own secret jeep training, I aced this one.

Eventually, we were given duties: KP—kitchen patrol—latrine cleaning, painting the barracks. I have to say, nearly all the assignments in Boot Camp were inhospitable.

It was September 19, 1952. I'd been "in" for eight weeks and finally was done. I was awarded Airman Third Class (A/3C), given a single stripe to sew onto my shoulder, and a duffle bag. Now the wait for a real assignment. I was eighteen years old and couldn't even express the excitement I was feeling.

A week went by. Another week. The excitement began to blur. I even worried they might have forgotten about me. Finally, orders came on October 1. I was to report to Keesler Air Force Base in Biloxi, Mississippi, for control tower training.

The only thing I knew about Mississippi was how to spell it. I also knew that it was a two-day train ride away. To think—I'd never even been outside New England.

I was booked in a sleeper car, which gave me time to read the newspapers I'd bought at the station, and time to think. I was really in the service! This was big, of course, but somewhat edgy too. I couldn't help but reflect on the not-too-distant news we read and talked about every single day. Normandy and the many servicemen who died there, fighting an evil tyrant. It all came out right; the tyrant was dead and Germany was on the mend. And yet. We had more tyrants to be wary of, in particular Kim Il Sung in Korea.

In June of 1950, the US and the UN went to war against him with the intent of maintaining democracy in East Asia. Suppose I'd be sent there? I was ready to go, of course, but I was apprehensive, too. Later I learned the graduating class just after mine was indeed sent there. Between us and the Soviet Union, China, and North Korea, ferocious air battles were fought even as I sat on the train. It was a war I followed intently. To be fair, we all did, and there was never a mission that didn't go unacknowledged. We cheered and ya-hooed and cried for every one of those boys as each bit of news came our way.

The train waddled on, through rolling hills, fields of wheat, soybeans and corn, and stopped in, what finally felt like, *The South*. I stepped outside and became intimately acquainted with how sweaty it felt here, sultry and slow.

An Air Force bus then took me to the OR (Orderly Room) on the base, where I'd be stationed for three more months to learn everything about Control Tower Operations.

February 19, 1953. At the bulletin board, I ran my finger down the alpha list, stopping at "Langway." Next to my name was a column titled PCS—Permanent Change of Station. I loved that word, "Permanent." Where: Williams Air Force Base, Chandler, Arizona. Second column: "Report to OR immediately." Thrilled, yet nervous, I hurried over for my orders: Report to 1903-3 AACS, no later than 23FEB53. A bunch of military jargon that basically said I was on my way to Airway and Air Communication Services.

What I knew of Arizona was: hot, cacti, cowboys, the Grand Canyon. How or where all this sorted itself out was anyone's guess, but I was primed, and I had four days to get ready to do it. I believe I repacked my duffle bag six times. Socks on top; no, socks at the bottom; papers on top. No, papers in an attaché, something slick-looking from the PX (a "post exchange," the US military's retail center). . .

I won't lie. I was disappointed that my sleeper car was replaced by second class benches requiring me to sit up straight for the entire trip. I arrived in the Big Easy just as the sun was lowering. I stepped down long enough to say my feet had touched the soil of New Orleans, then off to San Antonio. I sure learned how big the Lone Star State was in the forty hours it took to get across it. Not to mention the straight-jacket position I kept all the way through to Phoenix.

Reporting to the Staff Sergeant at Williams AF Base, as I was required to do, I was disheartened to learn that it was one more hurry-up-and-wait instance. The OJT (On-the-Job Training) at the control tower was overstaffed. I should check the bulletin board, though, every day for further instructions.

Now, waiting was not one of my fortes, and a new friend, a man who'd stay my friend for a good long time, Jan, told me not to hold my breath. It took him three months to get his control tower assignment. He told me I'd likely be ordered off base to the DFS (Directional Finding Station), which proved to be true.

Pilots needed to learn to bring their planes in without radar. Although completely unnecessary during peacetime—pilots don't lose their direction—I understood this to be an important lesson. What if something did happen and all they had was a handheld compass? What if there was zero visibility and an engine went out? To guide them in, we bounced radio signals off their aircraft, giving us enough information to direct them to land. Learning this was a good bit of fun.

A number of fighter jets were in commission at that time. The North American Aviation T-28, for example, and the Lockheed F-80, were both developed for the Second World War. Still used in acrobatic performances, in 1952, we used them for training. A jet would fly out from, say, the north with a flag on a cable extended off the back. Another jet, coming from the south, used that flag for target practice. Bam! Bam! Bam! Bam! The flag disintegrated.

Once, as Ma so often said, "It's all fun and games, you know. . ." a pilot flew too close to his target and got tangled in the cable, after which he couldn't open his landing gear and had to belly-land on the tarmac. They had to spray foam onto the runway to minimize the damage. But still!

When there was slack in time, we hung out with pretty girls, which there were plenty of in Phoenix, both high school and college aged. D-1 ranked Arizona State football games on Saturdays with no shortage of straight up belly-laughs made for great weekends. Then there was the Coffee Shack. Girls, guys in souped-up cars, a jukebox with the latest artists—Hank Williams, Frank Sinatra, Merle Haggard—and we were all the next expert at the jitterbug with no lack of partners to do it with.

Not only did our civilian friends arrive with custom hotrods, we had a few of our own. One guy named Al apparently had a money tree in his backyard, because one morning as we were lying on our bunks reading MAD Magazines, Al asked if I'd like to go into town. He had an idea. The answer was, of course, yes. We jumped into our civvies and caught the next bus.

Al pointed out a car dealership on the road and asked the driver to let us off. Without saying what he had in mind, he marched me over to a spit-shined red Ford Crestline convertible, the hottest thing going. Leaning over its side, inspecting the black leather and chrome, Al asked, "Well, wha'dya think?"

"What do I *think*, Al? What do I think? It's absolutely the most gorgeous piece of equipment this side of Hollywood!"

That was Saturday. On Monday, Al drove onto base in that very automobile, slick as can be. And boy oh boy, was he a hit at the Coffee Shack! The waitstaff, customers, even the owner came out to admire it. A month later, Al returned from Chicago, where he'd gone on leave, with a brand-new Harley Davidson cushioned and wrapped tight into the back seat of that convertible. Oh, and that bike was chartreuse. Chartreuse! A color so green, you'd have to say it in French to get it right.

The road to Chandler was a straight shot, no curves, no stop signs, nothing but horizon all around. Alongside the road ran two farmers' ditches with about five feet of water. Randy was driving his coupe, Jan sat in the middle and I was at the passenger end of his bench seat. Rocking out to "Your Cheatin' Heart" at top volume, we saw a train a few miles off, looking like a toy. As it grew larger, Randy didn't seem to be doing much about that fact. And we kept singing.

The train was a football field away. Still, Randy did nothing. But he looked worried. Suddenly, he yelled, "No brakes!"

"Downshift!" Jan shouted.

The next thing I knew the car was on its side in the ditchwater and I was in a world of pain, two big fellows lying on top of me with my arm crushed against the window crank. An ambulance quickly appeared and took us to the base hospital. Nothing (the X-ray showed) was broken, but my arm looked like a giant eggplant and hurt to the dickens.

It was not long before I had to say goodbye to my buddies. Orders were, I was being transferred one hundred miles to the south: Tucson, Davis-Monthan AF Base. Jan and Randy went too; that was a blessing. But sadly, all the other guys, Al included, were left behind.

The land around Tucson is called "enchanted" for good reason. The changing light, the startling green of saguaro cacti in juxtaposition, is nothing if not magical. We found a trail in the Superstition Mountains that became our favorite hike. At the summit was a lake as blue as a cat-eye marble that we named "Crater Lake," although, judging from its shape, round as a frypan, it could have been the blown top of a volcano. There were cliffs surrounding the lake that we dove from. Each time I did, I said a little prayer for Eddie, knowing if he was out there, he'd be proud of me now.

Full moon nights saw us at the lake with a cooler of A-1 Pilsners and some PBJs. We'd swim a little, drink a little, stare at the stars a lot, and talk all night as we watched the sky spread its glory from wispy blue to beating-heart crimson to indigo and violet. Then, we'd watch it drift back to orange, yellow and daylight. Life seemed to provide all its answers during those unforgettable all-nighters, like "time out of time."

One day while Jan and I were sauntering down a Tucson side street, we heard music coming out from what looked to be a gas station. "Let's check it out," I suggested, and we took a sharp right, right in through the back door.

I said to myself, *She's an impostor.* But her voice! I whispered to Jan. "Is that who I think it is?"

"I think that's who you think it is!"

It took no time for us to find a partner and start dancing up a storm. It was Helen O'Connell, singing one of our favorite tunes, "Tangerine." Whoever said the military was boring got it so very wrong. We seemed to be in the right place at the right time. Always. That night as we rode the bus back, our spirits were soaring. The number-one starlet, right here in Tucson, and we got to see her up front and in person!

Walking to the barracks, I stopped at the PX, quick, before turning it. Nothing was going on, the place quiet and dark, but a flutter on the bulletin board grabbed my attention. It was a newspaper clipping that I stopped to read. A car accident involving two airmen. Nellis AF Base in Las Vegas. The car was totaled. Funny, but the car in the photo looked exactly like the one my brother Paul had bought with his gambling winnings only weeks before, a 1953 Ford Mainliner hard top.

I did a double-take. It was Paul's car! My first thought: *Was he okay?* My second thought: *How the heck did he manage a car wreck a week after mine?* Third thought: *It was his last day of service.* I hoped to God he was okay. Not something our mother should have to hear. I took leave, went to see him, and, like me, he was banged up. But nothing serious.

Six more months; the days were like the heat, relentlessly redundant. Once a week I checked the bulletin board. Jan's prediction was spot-on: nothing, over and over. I knew enough about air traffic control orders that I could give them blindfolded. And yet, nothing.

It was now March, 1954. The Korean War was over by nearly a year, and still no word about where I was going. March 2, then 3. . . the weekend rolled in. Jan, Randy, and I took turns checking the bulletin board. Mondays were my day. I sauntered over after finishing the newspaper, not expecting much. And there it was. All three of our names: Jan Adams, Randy Hempton, Robert Langway. PCS (permanent change of station). Sidi Slimane, Morocco.

I didn't even know where to find those jokers at the moment; I was so excited with no one to tell, I just walked about, telling anyone who'd listen, "I'm off to *Africa!*" I'd never even flown on a plane before, let alone I was going with my two closest friends, let alone to a continent I knew nothing about!

Our orders to report to Camp Kilmer in New Jersey happened to coincide with America's favorite basketball season, "March Madness." And Camp Kilmer happened to be right near New York City. Well, Jan's darling team was Pittsburgh's Duchesne University, just across the river from the city in Ohio where he grew up. Mine, of course, was Holy Cross in Worcester. But the two teams were playing each other! In New York!

There was no way we'd miss this opportunity to rip each other a new one. I'd learned acronyms now to the point I used them in my dreams. Madison Square Garden was, naturally, MSG. And this was where we parked our bodies that Saturday, March 13. Holy Cross beat those knuckle-heads 71 to 62. Jan didn't hear the end of that until long after we'd arrived in Casablanca when we had better things to argue about.

I learned so many new things about my new country, Morocco, in such a short span, I could have been a tour guide. I learned that the first university in the world was founded in Fez by a woman in the year 859. It's still functioning as a school. I learned that Morocco was the first country to recognize the United States as an independent country, in 1777. Our war against Britain didn't even officially end until 1783. I learned two versions of the meaning of "Sahara." It's a tautology, first. Sahara in Arabic means "desert." It's like saying "Table Mesa." There's another version, perhaps the origin of the Arabic word, though: "Saha" meaning "thank you" in Berber, and "Ra" is the Egyptian Sun God. "Thank you, Sun." Lovely.

I was a noncommissioned officer by now and had grown from a shrimpy five-foot-nine to six foot tall. Evidently the Air Force was doing something right by me. My official duties at Nouasseur Tower began promptly at 1200, 1700, or 0700 the following morning, a seven-hour shift. It was a job full of responsibility with rarely a dull moment.

Berrechid is a Berber village five miles south of Nouasseur. Pilots often used it to report their positions when calling for landing instructions. One quiet Sunday afternoon, I was startled by a call from a jet flying in from Lakenheath, England. "Nouasseur Tower. Hello!! This is one lonely F-86 pilot from foggy England ready to pancake onto your runway. Flying over Bear Shit as we speak."

"I assure you, Sir, there is no bear shit in all of Casablanca," I replied. "However, upon landing, I can advise, you may encounter a bit of bull."

Without a moment's hesitation, he answered, "Roger that." It's how it was in the service. Joking was all the norm.

It was becoming clear however, this job was serious, messing around aside, and this was made all the more evident on the day I gave the "all-clear" without permission.

A squadron of B-36s was arriving from the States that day. The largest aircraft in the Airforce with a wingspan three-quarters the length of a football field and equipped to carry nuclear bombs. To see an entire squadron land was an exciting proposition, to say the least.

I started my shift at 1200, checked my flight strips and sat back in anticipation. At 1230 a C-54 cargo plane unexpectedly radioed, "Incoming." Our single runway was empty and I gave him permission to land, which he did, but what I saw from my tower was not good. The plane wobbled, then came to a full stop. From the distressed radio messages, I gathered the pilot had punctured a tire and was incapacitated. This required me to close the runway, so I sent out the NOTAM (Notice to Airmen) that all outbound and inbound flights were canceled.

At 1250, I received a radio message from the first B-36 requesting landing instructions; he was ten minutes out. I advised the pilot that the runway was closed.

"Roger that," he answered. However, he'd been flying for fourteen hours all the way from Puerto Rico, and apparently didn't like that order, because he ignored it. I watched the C-54 get its tire refitted and taxi away, when the B-36 radioed again saying he was in final approach. No clearance had yet been given, but I saw that the C-54 had left the runway. Another message from pilot B-36, "Landing approval needed ASAP. Over."

"Clear to land," I radioed back. The tower clock read 1300 hours. The landing happened, no incidents, and I watched on as one B-36 after another brought the day to completion.

The following morning, at "zero dark thirty" as they say, my first sergeant came to my hut to announce the commanding officer needed a word with me. This didn't sound good. I dressed and walked into his office at 0655. I saluted, to which he invited me to have a seat.

"Langway," he said. "I understand you gave the 'clear to land' to a B-36 bomber on a closed runway. Do you understand what that means to a bomber carrying explosives? That runway was to be opened by one officer and one officer alone, the AO. Are you the AO?"

"No, Sir. I am not."

"I didn't think so. I have a report to make to HQ that you've been reprimanded and that administrative actions have been taken. I hereby order you to write a thousand-word essay. About responsibility. Is that understood?"

"It is, Sir!"

"And, keep it together, Langway. You can do it."

"Yes, Sir. I can do it!"

He seemed like a man with a sense of humor, and I took my chances. I saluted, turned, and as I left, I said, "Sir? I've got it covered. Like a toothpick in a club sandwich."

He saluted and I swear his upper lip twitched into a grin. I swear he winked.

That essay was hard, though. I thought back to my "essay" in the third grade when Mrs. Fields made me write "I will be a good citizen" five hundred times after I shot a spitball at Shirley's braid but missed, and it landed on Mrs. Fields's open textbook. Being a "good citizen" wasn't going to fly here, however. I stressed, I drank a couple of beers, and by the time the night was over, I had that paper type-written, with no mistakes, on the CO's desk by 0700.

"A rare locust invasion is headed your way, Sir, arriving from the south," the tower chief informed me one morning.

"Yes, Sir," I saluted. "And, Sir? What exactly does a locust look like?"

"Wingspan's about equal to a dingbat," he knuckled me on the forehead.

"Roger that!" I answered and realized he was serious. These were *grasshoppers* he was talking about, coming our way, in swarms.

At 1200 my shift started. At 1245, a single locust crossed my window. 1246, another dozen. My first landing radioed in. It was a troop transport plane, a C-47, about ten minutes out. I gave the weather conditions and landing instructions, but before ending, I asked if he couldn't fly south of the airfield to see if there was something called "a swarm." Five minutes later he radioed, "Nouasseur Tower. A swarm detected. Hundreds of thousands, by my estimation. Eight miles to the south. Headed your way."

"Roger that," I responded and gave landing instructions to fly in from the north. Within fifteen minutes my entire window was splattered with locust carcasses. I went outside to clean it and found the stairs awash in crunchy exoskeletons. The sky was darkened. It occurred to me these dead bugs could be a source of danger to my pilots. A landing strip covered in bug slime could cause an aircraft to slide off course, and flying bugs could cause the visibility to go to zero. I radared all personnel that the runway, inbound and outbound, was closed until further notice.

The swarm came and went, moving on to England where they died on the beaches and city streets, causing damage to thousands of miles of croplands. It turned out to be the famous "Year of the Locust," 1954.

Locust swarms usually originate in northern Africa or the Middle East and can cover as much as one-fifth of the Earth's surface at one time, eating its weight in plants in a single day. In other words, a swarm the size of London can eat the same amount that half the population of England does before sundown. Mythologically considered a sign of descending doom, swarms have been reported since the time of the Pharaohs. I considered them to be a colossal mess.

That day, however, gave me a new understanding of something I'd learned from a merchant in the medina: "Everything's possible in Morocco; nothing is certain."

9

Adieu

URSULA

JUNE, 1953

It had been nearly a month since my family left. I'd been so busy with my studies, hoping to pass "le bac," I hardly noticed. The *baccalauréat professionnel* was a huge exam, life-changing, if I passed it. It would test me on general scholarly issues as well as industry standards for various professions. I wanted to be a translator, perhaps work for an embassy somewhere. I was also starting as a part-time student at Alliance Française, believing if I could master the language, master the mannerisms, I could confidently live the rest of my life as a bonafide "Parisienne."

For *le bac*, there would be a graduation and a small ceremony with speeches. What began to pull at my heart was not that my Maman would not be there, or that little Yves and Mimi were growing up and I wouldn't hear their sweet voices saying, *"felicitations"* and *"bonne chance"* at their big sister's rite of passage, or that Claude-Elie would be my only witness. What pulled at my heart was that I wanted more, and somehow Paris and Alliance Française and all the languages I'd learned and experiences I'd had, were just not enough. I couldn't put my finger on it. What was not enough?

August 6, 1953. My birthday came on a Thursday that year. My day at the Burrough's Corporation should have felt like drudgery, yet it was anything but. I had plans with Claude-Elie on Saturday, only two days away. Like every Saturday, we planned a picnic at the Bois de Boulogne.

The Bois, once a hunting ground for the nobility, had been decimated during the final siege of Paris when Napoleon Bonaparte made his final flight into exile. At the time, thousands of trees had been cut for firewood and shelters for the left-behind soldiers, and for decades after, the land was a barren moonscape of rotting stumps and stagnant, algae-infested ponds, a place rife with robberies and unsolved murders. Today there are thousands of trees in the Bois. A giant sequoia imported from California and the whimsical Monkey Puzzle tree from Chile are but a few. Within the park are two man-made lakes connected by a stream, and all this was created on 2,000 acres, three times the size of London's Hyde Park, Napoleon III's inspiration for this magical land Claude-Elie and I called "our Saturday place."

Only one more day of work, I kept humming to myself. On my way home, I stopped at the newspaper kiosk and bought myself nineteen red roses and a copy of *Le Figaro*, which I planned to read with my evening tea. And then just one more day.

We met early on Saturday, promising even our coffees would start at the Métro to get the most of the day. At the lower of the two lakes, "le Grand," we rented a rowboat—once a sport allowed only for the nobility—and rowed in the direction of the small island on which sat the restaurant called Chalet des Îles. As we rowed, I told Claude-Elie all about passing *le bac* to which Claude-Elie smiled broadly.

"I have something for you," she said, "to celebrate all of it: you, your birthday, your accomplishments, your future." From her clutch purse she coyly produced a small box wrapped in silver foil and handed it to me.

"Open it!" she exclaimed. "Open it!"

We never exchanged gifts. I fingered the paper, careful not to tear it, and simply muttered, "My gosh, Claude-Elie. I'm overwhelmed!"

Claude-Elie looked at me pensively and said, "Ursula, you mean so much to me. And now your life is moving along. While mine? I can't say, really. My Papa makes life so difficult. My only wish is not to be near him. My Maman? She is gone. I cannot help that. The school? It is so uninteresting to me. I have no high hopes of passing *le bac*. But you, Ursula. . . you will go places. I feel so happy for you."

Her truth made me sad for her and a bit worried too. Was she predicting something? She was right about one thing. She would not pass *le bac*. But it was my birthday. I shook off my concerns and proceeded to open her gift. Out of the box, I pulled a thin silver bracelet from which dangled a small charm in the shape of two clutching hands. I tried to fix the clasp around my wrist without showing the tears in my eyes. It was such a meaningful gift.

"Every year," Claude-Elie said with gleaming eyes, "we'll have something special and every year, I'll give you a new charm. This one is for our friendship. . . may it last forever!"

"Oh, Claude-Elie," I said. "But I must give you one too. That way we can wish each other something new every year!"

"*D'accord!*" she exclaimed.

Just then, a rowboat passed by us with a small boy in shorts and a smart button-down shirt leaning over the side and waving his little arm as if to salute us. "It's a fish! It's a fish! Look! *Un poisson très gros!*" he shouted. His eyes were wide as two francs, and his excitement made us giggle. Behind him sat his Papa, who hesitated only for a moment, then went back to his story of a fish and its home ". . .under the deep, deep sea, where mermaids live. There, there is a house, much like a cave, that is full of bright lights and colors. . ." On and on he went, the child evermore enchanted. Then slowly our boats drifted apart.

The boy, the Papa, the story of the fish, came and went, like a feeling. Claude-Elie and I sat then for a long moment, allowing the sun and the lapping lake to still our thoughts. "You know," Claude-Elie said dreamily. "I wish I had had a Papa like that. One who'd tell me stories. Who was kind, maybe let me sit on his lap just once. . ."

"Who would tell you about mermaids that lived in le Grand?" I added, jokingly. But Claude-Elie's mood was melancholic.

"I only wish for just one day when he's not the foul ogre he is. Just one day. . . Do you know? I was locked inside the pantry. For hours, he left me there as punishment, nothing but a crack of light and bags of flour and beans and the smell of Madame Caillou. And she? She just stood by, gloating. It was all because I came home with my coat unbuttoned. It was warm out! I didn't want my coat buttoned! He hit me with his umbrella first, then chased me into the pantry. And she? Just gawked, like the fat old hussy she is."

I had to laugh. Claude-Elie (I never called her just "Claude"— it offended her as it reminded her of a neighbor who'd "betrayed" her on more than one occasion) could make me laugh at nothing at all.

"Claude-Elie," I said, in all earnestness. "Does it help you to know I haven't seen my father since I was four? My real father, I mean. I can barely picture what he looks like anymore. I only remember the tweed of his coat as he walked away. We were in Milan then. I have not felt the kindness of a Papa since that day, that last hug when he told me to be '*brav.*' I have not felt the joy of that little garçon and his fish. . . in, oh, so long. . ."

"Ah, but we are a pair, aren't we? What will become of us?" Claude-Elie pulled a few strands of hair from her lip and looked closely as if checking for split ends, then answered herself. "I want to be a pilot, you know? I could fly and fly and even fly to Buenos Aires! Or Portugal! But no," she looked to the lacy treetops above and pinched her lips. "Papa said no. Why? 'You're too stupid,' he told me. He's right. I've no ambition to pass the baccaulauréat. Not now, while I still live with him and his wife. He said the best I could hope to be is a stewardess, like Mme Boucher from the apartment next door, the woman he says is a *salope*."

"Claude-Elie," I broke in. "You must absolutely do it! Forget your father. I too dream of things. So many things. I wanted to be a dancer once. . ." Somehow, just voicing this dream so long kept secret inside me, brought up the urge of tears. But I dismissed it.

We sat then, our oars lying still at the side of the boat, both of us realizing a truth. We were living a life that all the "if-onlys" couldn't change. "One thing I know, though, is I'll never be like those women at the Burrough's Corporation. 'M. This and M. That,' and 'can I bring you a coffee, M. So-and-So,' or even worse. Mlle Lafromboise with her, 'a little something brown, Monsieur?,' meaning the cognac that sits in his liquor roll-away, and with a wink disappearing into his office with him. It sickens me how all they want, these so-called secretaries, is to marry one of them. THAT I will never aspire to. Not me! I want a real career, something I can be proud of. I just turn my head and crank another sheet of paper and a carbon into my typewriter, and try to look very, very busy."

We had drifted under a bridge and sat in our rowboat completely still, as if in the doldrums. I peered at my wrist, the new bracelet that sparkled off my skin, the two hands—our two hands—embraced. I vowed to buy her a gift of the same for the birthday she had coming up, also her nineteenth. The charm I'd buy her would unquestionably be an airplane, something I hoped she would, but knew innately she'd never fly.

That night I walked home admiring the full moon above Paris. Is it the same in Casablanca? I wondered, and suddenly missed my two siblings. Oh, how they must have grown by now! Mimi? Three years old? Four? And Yves! What would he make of the donkey carts and snake charmers in his new world?

I opened the door to my apartment; it felt dark and empty. I tore a few sheets from *Le Figaro* and started a fire in the hearth, then plunked down in the only spot there was, an overstuffed armchair, and picked at the antimacassar on the armrest. As I stared into the fire, I contemplated my life, all nineteen years of it. The schools and teachers, languages and cultures, a war I had no reference for. I breathed deep and said a little prayer of thanks. True. I was only nineteen. But I was nineteen! Somewhere within me, an inspiration was bubbling to life. I felt it more than thought it, but it was a knowing: I was in for something big. I pulled a blanket over me and drifted into a deep sleep right there at the fire.

JACQUE

This New Life

JUNE, 1953

It was a white, button-shirt with gold cufflinks that he wore that first day, something he'd purchased at Galeries Lafayette Haussmann in Paris's 9th arrondissement with money from their savings. Jacque had shopped alone, not telling anyone, but stood in the parlor that evening, modeling the shirt with its tight fit and starched collar. It did not go unnoticed that his shopping spree took place only a three-minute walk from the Burroughs Corporation. Could he have stopped in to say hello? *May I take you for a coffee?* No, nothing was ever said that Ursula, too, contributed to paying the heat bill and to buying the baguettes and milk on her way home.

But the shirt. The shirt was everything. What he would wear the first new day in Casablanca at his prestigious new job, head of the sales department at the Coca-Cola Company.

In Africa

After the Second World War, Coca-Cola began to invest in a large-scale distribution effort throughout the African continent. Starting in South Africa long before the war, Coca-Cola now quickly spread to Algeria, Egypt, and Morocco. From there, the business model was to move quickly into the lower countries as well: Nigeria, Ghana, Kenya, and Rhodesia. It was this grand plan that Jacque Guerin had been invited to promote. The opportunity before him was breath-taking, the potential accounts limitless.

The offices were stark. The colors were bold red against a blinding white. Bright, overhead lights illuminated the hallways that were lined with important-looking glass-enclosed offices. Jacque arrived that first day, cheeks as fresh as his dapper suit and cufflinked shirt. His suntanned hands with their polished nails shook those of each of his higher-ups with great enthusiasm. Yes, he was prepared, joking with only slight innuendos and an air of confidence. He did not let on that it was a "red taxi"—a shared, thus cheap, taxi—that he took to the office that day. He did not yet own a car, something he secretly blamed his wife for: Were it not for these children and housekeepers and oh, the furniture! What all she said she needed! If it were not for all that, he'd be well up on the ladder to success.

ELEANOR
This New Life

For Eleanor, Casablanca was less an opportunity as it was a chimera. Her heart was back in Paris, but her loyalty was to her chosen life with her new husband and two children. On the quiet Rue Dunkerque, the Guerins made their home on the second floor of a stuccoed apartment building with latticed wood shutters, the garden pungent with jasmine.

Eleanor quickly busied herself finding the best day schools for children of French-speaking Europeans. There were many. She set about finding a housemaid and acquainting herself with the local souks (the small shops that catered their single item for sale). The butcher shop, for instance, was but a narrow counter behind which a thin man in a fez stood, the shank of a cow hanging from a ceiling hook by his side. Behind him, attached to the wall, was an array of knives and cleavers as well as choice cuts of lamb, also hanging from ceiling hooks. Next door was an olive shop with wicker platters out front displaying conical piles of olives in colors ranging from eggplant-purple to turmeric-yellow. Further along in the medina were the vegetable souks. Onions, green onions, red onions, chilis, tomatoes, carrots, parsley, cabbage, potatoes, garlic. And further down, along a narrow, cobbled alleyway, was where the home furnishings were: brass lamps with tiny star-shaped cutouts and teapots like small copulas with long spouts, rugs and wall hangings, bed coverings and pillows. It took no time for Eleanor to become enamored with her new world.

There was one thing missing though. She missed her daughter, the girl who could brighten even the sulkiest day. Yes, she missed Ursula terribly. And there was a second hole in her heart—the lack of something to do.

Back in London she held a worthy job, one that paid well and she, a woman, stood out among her co-workers, recognized for her quick wit and ease with languages. In Casablanca? Not so much. Clearly, her place in this place was "in the home."

With some coaxing from Zora (the maid who knew everything about Casablanca and even a little about what a newly-arrived French woman would want), Eleanor learned to make her way, most afternoons, to the rooftop terrace of the Hôtel Central for a mint tea and halwa. Here she eventually met others who were like her—from France and other countries in Europe—women who, too, seemed out of place in Morocco. "Why, it's impossible to find a glass of decent wine around here!" one complained. "And the baguettes! Abysmal!"

It's not the fault of the Moroccans, Eleanor thought. *Try the chebakia, for God's sake*, she wanted to argue. But she was in a foreign place, one she didn't have her bearings in just yet. She simply stayed silent and sipped her tea.

When evening came and the children were bathed and dressed for dinner, Eleanor freshly made-up for her husband, a man bleary from hours of kibitzing in rooms filled with cigarette smoke and boring conversation, they often found they had little to talk about. His work didn't sound all that exciting; her day did not interest him. Then there was the day he arrived early with a bundle of Damascus roses to kiss her square on the lips. He'd received his first bonus, a check large enough to buy the slightly-used Citroën he'd had his eyes on.

Jacque sat easily in his armchair, removed a cigarette from its pack, and put it to his lips. He loosened his tie, lit the cigarette, inhaled deeply and blew smoke through his nostrils, then flicked the ash into his waiting ashtray. "They awarded me," he said then, eyeing her. *Did she understand what this meant?* "It was quite the ceremony. At the board meeting. I was called to the head of the conference table." He leaned his head back and closed his eyes as if he were recalling the entire episode. "Oh, how everyone's eyes followed as I walked up! Can you believe it, Eleanor? An *award*!"

Eleanor did not answer immediately. Instead, she rose to empty his ashtray and deliver it back to him, cleaned. "How interesting," she said. She tried hard to share in his cheerfulness and even suggested champagne. But Jacque noticed the distance in her demeanor, and this annoyed him. What he wanted was her recognition, praise for all he was about to be. Joy for the places he was going.

They talked on in fits and starts. He pulled out another cigarette and lit it, the smoke making a blue haze around his head.

That night, they toasted their glasses in silence, then went off to bed.

URSULA

A Sharp Turn of Events

It was September now, the end of it, really. The leaves were brilliant this year, and on most days, I chose to walk to work, just to hear the rustle of my shoes kicking through the wind-blown piles that had not yet been swept up.

It was a Monday, when at the Burrough's Corporation I was handed a telegram immediately upon arriving. It was stamped "Casablanca." I could not believe my eyes. From Africa, a note for me? It was short as was common for telegrams: less than one hundred characters. "We send love. STOP. Mimi says Bonjour. STOP. Yves shows his toy boat. STOP. We miss you, ma chére! STOP." Oh my, how my heart fluttered and everyone wanted to know how it was I had people in such a far-off place. I was confused. I thought everyone knew.

"My stepfather was offered a big job he couldn't decline. My parents and two siblings moved to Casablanca for that reason. They must be doing well! I'm so happy for them."

"Will you be joining them?" Everyone wanted to know.

I did not have an answer, but I wondered the same.

That night I vowed to write a long letter. I'd tell Maman all about my progress at Alliance Française and the wonderful times spent with Claude-Elie, how I barely knew that time was passing. How I hoped she and her husband (I still couldn't bring myself to call him anything more. I'm so sorry, Maman) were happy in Morocco and oh, how I couldn't wait to see them. . . when are you coming back?

It was never mentioned before they left. It was just assumed we'd be together again. But now I wondered about that promise.

I didn't know what to think, so I didn't think. Instead, I wrote it all into that letter. I reread it, crossed out a few things and added some lines, then sealed the blue airmail paper and left it for the morning when I'd take it to the post office, a slice of my heart going too, as it dropped into the yellow letter box.

I professed, then, to make a habit of writing "home," whether I heard back or not. And this promise made me feel good, like a big sister and a loving daughter. I became enthused to finish my French business training at the Alliance Française. I was going to get that prestigious position Claude-Elie and I had talked about in the boat. And somehow, sometime soon, I'd see my family again.

Autumn turned to slush quickly once November arrived. Gray skies, and a never-ending trudge to the Métro to get to work. Claude-Elie and I now spent our weekends at the Louvre, bringing our own sandwiches to eat and a hot tea to drink on one of the benches off in the many side rooms.

We stood before the Venus de Milo one day when Claude-Elie nearly tripped over a girl who was standing beside her. Apologies and, "Pardon! Pardon!" when Claude-Elie looked curiously at her counterpart. "Francine?"

"Oui!"

"Is it really you?"

"But, oui, it is! My dear Claude-Elie! But where have you been?"

Francine and Claude-Elie, I would soon learn, had been childhood friends when Claude-Elie's mother was still alive. In fact, their mothers were neighbors, taking the two girls for strolls in the Bois de Vincennes and tea on the Champs-Élysées. But this I could not know. I only saw how much the two looked alike: aquiline bone structure, thick hair and an upright posture.

"You must join us, Francine! This is my dear friend, Ursula.

She's just like us. We're friends forever! Do come! We were on our way to the Left Bank for a coffee at Café de Flore. Do join us?"

It proved to be a surface friendship, friendly but not of substance. Francine and Claude-Elie had history, and so now it would be the three of us, but the days on the lake, sharing our deepest secrets? That would not take place, not with Francine. She came from a "good" family. Her parents shared in her secrets and praised her accomplishments. She didn't have the loss Claude-Elie and I felt: Claude-Elie with her mean-spirited father and a mother who was dead. Me with a family an entire continent away.

I did not want Christmas, alone for the first time, to be a problem, and that was something that was quickly solved: Claude-Elie and I were invited to the table at Francine's home for Christmas Eve. I bought myself a maroon velvet dress with a flared skirt and black wool collar with matching pumps, all the fashion in 1953. I purchased some small gifts—an ornament for their tree, a *bûche de Noël*—a scrumptious chocolate cake in the shape of a yule log—and a bottle of rosé. It was only a week away, but an evening I was looking forward to.

Given it was winter now, the solstice in fact, I walked home in the dark. I made a quick dinner and fell into bed. That night I had a terrifying dream that woke me with the jitters. It was Jacque who appeared in my dream, of all people. In the dream, I felt sorry for him and kept trying to console him. But he was crying so hard it was difficult to understand what he was trying to say. His hands. They kept flitting around his head. Then, in a moment of clarity—I mean real clarity, like only in a dream would you know this—he looked at me with a fresh wet face and eyes that were bright and large like a puppy, and terrified. "Your mother's leaving me," he mumbled, spittle bubbling from his mouth.

That was the end of the dream. How strange, I thought. If it were anything, it would be she who'd weep, not he.

The official end to the Christmas holidays was January sixth, when I finally went back to work. That day, an unusual thing occurred. I was notified that, given the Burrough's Corporation, given that we had telecommunications with all the French colonies, there was a call about to be put through, for me, from Casablanca.

This did not sound good.

I was to wait at the main reception telephone where the operator would put through the call coming from la Poste Centrale in Casablanca. Sometimes this process took hours.

I waited. I breathed. I had a coffee. I asked the secretary if I could use her typewriter, to which she said, "Absolutely!" I needed to stay busy.

That call finally came through in the early afternoon, Maman on the line.

"Mami!" I said, like the child I was to her once. "Mami! How are you?" I knew the call was costing her a pretty penny. From what I understood, it was 350 francs for the first three minutes, a quarter of a week's paycheck.

Ursula." she said. A definitive statement. There was a long pause during which she breathed deeply. "I need you. Please. Come. . ."

"But, Mami!? Why?"

"Jacque. . . Jacque. He left me. He's gone. Nothing, not even a note."

Maman was crying on the other end. I knew this because there was another long pause, one I knew she couldn't afford at 100 francs per minute.

"It happened Christmas Eve. I waited all night for him,

thinking the children wanted to open a present; we had a dinner prepared. Oh, Ursula! It's so terrible! He left for another woman! A Moroccan girl, no less!"

So many things roiled through my brain after that call. I missed my family, sure, and I should have been all too happy for this plea to rejoin them. And I was. But something quite different, and new, began to fester in my heart. Anger. Anger, first at that man for all he'd done to me and the turns my life took because of him. And then for what he'd done to Maman. Had he not entered our lives. . . oh, how things could have been so different.

Anger, now, too, at Maman. That I, once again, had to traipse behind her, always behind her, because of what she wanted. When would it be what I wanted? I never pictured our reunion to take place in Africa! Surely, it would be back here, in Paris, the city we both loved, and where we belonged. Why didn't *she* leave *him*? And come *home*? I quietly knew the answer. That had she left him, particularly in Morocco where women's rights were limited to a primary school education, she'd be left with nothing.

It would take several months and a bit of planning before I could make the move, not the least of which was the completion of my business courses at Alliance Française. There were other things too—liquidating the apartment, knowing what to keep and what to toss. And most heart-breaking of all: Claude-Elie. How to say goodbye to the person who'd been my other half for so many years.

It was Claude-Elie's idea. One afternoon, we took the Métro to Monoprix to purchase, for each other, a charm for our bracelets that would cement our friendship forever. It was a bright winter day, the kind where the sun and the sky merged into a singular luminous experience. We began our day with *chocolat chaud* and croissants at Café Flore, then made our way straight to the jewelry counter. I purchased a rainbow for her, and Claude-Elie gave me a ladybug. "The symbol of happiness," she told me.

It was March in 1954 when I gave my final glance to the apartment on Rue Raspail, locked the door, and handed the key to Mme Auclair, the landlady. What I traveled with was light: a few books, a handbag that held my diary and several pens, some writing paper, and a cloth shoulder bag with my clothes, which were not many. My new maroon Christmas dress that I'd spent a week's pay on, I gave to Claude-Elie as remembrance. Of course, she looked stunning in it.

I was to travel to Marseille by train, then by ship straight to Casablanca, the city of my mother, my sister and my brother. My family. As I boarded, I looked back and waved with my hanky. This was my goodbye to Paris, the city I had loved. And my goodbye to Claude-Elie. Just the thought that I might not see her again made me shudder. I could not think of it; it just couldn't be so. But I hopped up the steps and took my seat in the first-class compartment which allowed room for my bags. I sat by the window where I also had a small table on which I could write. Yes, I was saying goodbye to my past, but I was also saying goodbye to the country of France, a country I'd considered home for over four years, and hello to a new one, Morocco.

The 800-kilometer journey took most of the day. Watching the city diminish to a few scattered farmhouses, then the fallow snow-covered fields and small medieval villages roll along past my window, gave me much time to think. The train stopped in Lyon, where I hopped off just to say I'd been there. Off in the distance I could just barely see the dome of the Basilica de Notre Dame de Fourvière, and then the conductor announced we were pushing on.

The train began to climb and meander through what I learned from a fellow passenger were the vineyards of the Côtes du Rhône and the lovely medieval city of Avignon. With the rocking of the train and the beautiful vistas falling away, I realized this was a country I may never see again. I had fallen in love with Paris, but I'd also fallen in love with the people. Their easy-going manner was quite the contrast to the British nuns from my past.

But it was a new era. The war was behind us, and it was a time to reinvent. Yes, I was angry still. Morocco was not my choice. But I had *le bac* (which I aced), my French business studies were completed, and I knew who I was. If Claude-Elie were to be an example, I'd say I knew how to fly now. And with this knowledge tucked away, I was going to make Casablanca soar for me.

We arrived in Marseilles, where I quickly grabbed my belongings and made my way to the ship that would take me to Morocco. I felt prepared now. I had the train to thank for that. Even here, with forty more hours on the sea, my convictions kept whispering: *You'll find your way.*

All these dreams and plans did not prepare me, however, for who I saw standing before me on the platform when I arrived at the train station in Casablanca. Mimi with tall slender legs, a young lady already. And Yves! His blushing-blond locks had become fiery red and matched his freckles, precisely. His body had filled out; he looked like the tough three-year-old that he was. And oh, but they were the picture! The two were dressed in matching outfits with blue blazers and white blouses; Mimi had a white bow in her hair, Yves, a white bow tie. And behind them stood Maman, beaming. I was overcome with emotion. I dropped my bags, ran to them and held them tight, one then the other, Maman was last. I hugged her the longest. We were a family again.

As the taxi drove on narrow streets through crowded neighbor-hoods, Maman pointed out how much the homes here seemed hushed and secretive. "They're not showy, like the Parisiennes. Look there. The door, hidden. The windows are masked by shutters. It's because people here do not want to attract undue attention. Or envy."

"Rather telling of the culture, isn't it?" I said. I was captivated already. Things already were so different from what I'd known.

"But the insides! Wait till you see the insides! They lavish their homes with luxury—if they can afford it, of course—with thick rugs, gardens, tucked-away nooks to have one's tea. . ."

We arrived at her apartment. Rue Voltaire was quiet, the homes unassuming, most of them surrounded by walls over-hung with lush flowering things I did not have names for yet. Maman continued her quick lesson in Moroccan as she opened the door to her—now mine as well—apartment. Immediately I recognized the Moroccan influence: rugs, low brass lamps, low seating, and plush cushions all around.

"You'll have the second room, Ursula. There you'll have privacy and a chance to spread out. My room is the front room, views and all, and it's large. But it will accommodate all three of us: Anne-Marie, Yves, and me, of course."

It was spring back home in Paris. Here it felt like deep summer already. It would take some time to get used to this new life, the slow pace, the sweltering air, the flowering everything every-where, bougainvillea, orange trees and lemon trees, the medina, the men in their djellabas and fezes, the women with their hijabs. But I would stay true to the promise I made on my journey here: Casablanca will soar for me.

Maman had a job as an interpreter on the US Air Force base called Nouasseur, just outside of Casablanca. She loved her job, telling me often how good it was for her to use her language skills. "They can't believe I speak French and English. Of course I do. But that I speak German as well completely baffles them. I'd even learn Arabic, if I had the time."

Maman tended to talk a lot. And a lot about trivial things. I wanted to know the important stuff. I wanted to know about Jacque. Where was he? Would we run across him? Who *was* this woman he ran off with? These were questions whose answers were hard to tease out of her. She'd say one word: yes. Then move on to the subject at hand, which was never Jacque. What have we for dinner? Was I comfortable in her home? In time, bits and pieces made a mosaic of her life. She'd not been happy, all that much. At least that was clear. At least not at first, when they first came to Morocco.

"It's not easy," Maman explained one day. "Women here don't really work. I think Jacque fancied himself to have such a household: his woman at home, while he enjoys his new career." What I extrapolated? She bossed him, and he sulked. I imagined this new woman he ran off with to be younger, blushing, and obedient. Maman hinted that that could be true.

I, of course, was much like Maman in that I, too, wanted fulfillment. I was young, I was bright. I wanted work, and I knew I had a good amount to offer. I, too, spoke several languages and could communicate well in any one of them.

Maman must have had a lot to do with this, but, again, she was secretive. Only a month after I arrived, an official-looking note came home from work with her, saying I needed to interview with a certain "Captain White." Job description: must be able to read, write and converse in both French and English. Additional languages helpful, but not required. Please inquire at 0900 on Monday, 12 April.

It was Friday. I'd been spending my days walking the children—my siblings—to preschool and picking them up again in the afternoons. In between, I walked. I walked all over Casablanca, stopping for a coffee, then stopping at a mosque, where I felt obliged to cover my head with a scarf, although I was never asked. I believe the Moroccans were too polite to correct a French woman, or one who resembled French, but I wanted to do how they do. I covered my hair, kicked off my shoes at the entrance, and made my way to the women's side. There I dropped to my knees and admired my surroundings. The architecture was so unique. . . so ornate and intricately sculpted in patterns and designs. Nothing like the cathedrals I knew from home, from France or England, with their opulent crosses with images of an agonized Christ. Here there was none of that, and I wondered: Did their Mohammed not suffer? Their story was so similar to ours, a Messiah, a teaching, a history from the same part of the world—and yet the customs here were so different. Cover the head, wash the feet, pray five times a day. I rather loved the mystique of it all.

Now, here was an offer for a job with a real paycheck. I'd be able to contribute and help my mother. I could tell she was struggling now that Jacque's income was gone. At night after the little ones went to sleep, she'd pull out an accounting ledger and write down all her outlays that day: what Zora had spent at the market, the doctor's visit, the gardener. And then the trivialities: taxis, a purchase of flowers. Then there was the ongoing money that went to the school Yves and Mimi attended, the landlord's monthly payment. She kept a second log, a sort of wish-list of what she hoped to buy in the future—a wicker chaise for the balcony, a visit to the hammam, a gift of a new scarf for Zora. I knew from her knitted brows things did not always add up, and I was all too happy to help by at least taking some of the bullet points off her wish-list.

It was only a month since I'd arrived. I'd learned so much, already, it felt like I'd been here for a year. And now I'd had my interview with Captain White.

I could not wait to announce my news that night at dinner.

I'd just interviewed that day—I did not even tell Maman about the meeting as I wanted it to be a surprise. But here was the big surprise: I was hired on the spot and was to start in only a few days! I needed new shoes!

After we ate and I outlined what my days would look like in the upcoming weeks, Zora brought out the mint tea, spiced and sweetened with thyme and a large cube of sugar. "This Captain White seemed quite excited and the job responsibilities are quite extensive," I blabbered on. Maman suggested we move out to the terrace. She wanted a smoke, and most certainly wanted to know more about this new position. We talked and talked. She lit a second cigarette and then suggested we take in the warm evening for a stroll, something we did often, admiring the moon, the fragrances, the quiet of the streets at night.

"Are you happy here?"

Her question took me by surprise. I'd not been here long enough to formulate an opinion, so I said what I hoped would put her at ease. "Maman! Everything will be good. I'm about to start a job. We have a lovely apartment. My darling sister and brother are well taken care of. The issues with Jacque, they'll be resolved soon enough. And me? I miss Paris, yes. But now I have you. And I have my siblings. I have my family. This is all I ever wanted." I know this appeased her tremendously.

Our routine remained much the same, only it was Zora now who took the children to school. We took dinner early, around 5:00, served by Zora five days of the week, and often, after the children were laid to bed, Maman and I went to the street below, just to stroll. The summer had passed, although in Casablanca it was hardly noticeable. Everything seemed to bloom incessantly, and it only got hotter throughout the day. But we now had cooling breezes at night. It was on one of these evenings when the freshness of the African autumn wafted through the trees. A "barley moon" had risen and hung high above us while sea breezes floated from around darkened corners. We walked in the direction of the wharf. Maman smoked, and, unusually, there were silent periods between us, moments when I could think and she, I'm sure, was formulating some sort of new digression to talk about. After stomping out her cigarette on the pavement, she looked at me straight. "Ursula," she said. "We need to get out. Have some fun; meet some people."

Maman's boss had told her that the base often held dances for the enlisted men, and locals often showed up as well. " 'It can be quite a lot of fun,' he told me, and said they often had interesting local entertainment. . . What do you think?"

It was an unusual request. She was usually quite rigid, tight, needing order and a regiment. There was a time and a place for everything, and a night out on the town did not seem to fit that mold. She continued, "We've been apart for so long. I've been thinking about this. Life has put some strange obstacles in our path, mine, yours, mine again. But now, we're here, the two of us. Isn't it time?"

She took my hand in hers. We walked that way, in silence for a while and watched the moon. "Yes," she said, finally.

"Yes, it's time," she repeated. It was as if the wind had spoken.

10

Made in Heaven

 BOB

1954

The November air was crisp, a refuge after the sweltering Moroccan summer, the sky so blue it could have been a mirage. It was November 7, 1954, my first day seeing the beautiful woman I'd met only two days earlier. My palms were sweating.

I'd taken a city bus from the Air Force base to Place Lyautey, known colloquially as "pigeon square," where it was not uncommon to see children chasing after pigeons that swooped and fluttered around the fountain. I asked a peanut seller in my most eloquent French, "*Sauriez-vous où est le Rue Voltaire?*" I must have had "American" written all across my forehead because he answered in perfect English and pointed, "Rue Voltaire, sir, is in that direction, about two kilometers. You can't miss it."

His voice entered my head like a prophecy: *You can't miss it!* Then, all sorts of doubts flooded in: *Suppose I don't have the correct address; suppose I can't find it? What if she doesn't remember?*

As I walked in the direction he had pointed, I came upon a church as large as St. Patrick's Cathedral in New York. I was awestruck. This was a Muslim country. What was a cathedral doing here? When I asked a waiting taxi driver what the name was, he sniffed his nose in its direction and snorted, "*Cathédrale du Sacré-Coeur,*" and turned his head away. Apparently, he was not fond of it, as a few Moroccans were unimpressed with anything French.

From here it was easy to find Rue Voltaire, which turned out to be a quiet street with white, stuccoed buildings surrounded by privacy walls, nearly all of them draped in bougainvillea with colors so bright they looked fake. I looked for number four, and, as if a movie-set backdrop had plunged before me, there it stood, a sunny three-story house with black wrought-iron balconies across the front of each of the *porte-fenêtre* patio doors. It gave off a warm feeling, as though its sole purpose was to welcome me. But this could have been my imagination, an embellishment to that movie set, although it helped put my pounding heart at ease.

Inside the dark vestibule, Mme Guerin was listed in apartment A on the second floor, for which I took the box-elevator that dropped me directly at her door. "It's showtime!" I told myself, and rang the bell. To this day, my mind's eye will see that door swing open to reveal the most elegant woman I'd ever laid eyes on—movies included. She wore a white pleated skirt and a fitted turquoise blouse, turquoise earrings, white pumps, and her hair. . . her hair! It was radiant, golden, draping her shoulders in voluminous waves.

She smiled and kindly beckoned me in.

The home had a Moroccan feel to it, a large low-standing table surrounded by cushions atop a sort of bench that squared three sides of the room. On the walls hung framed photos of Paris—the Eiffel Tower and l'Arc de Triomphe—and a few with scenes of people at outdoor tables, watching as women with poodles on leashes walked by. The *zillij* tiled floor had scattered carpets, tastefully unmatched. It was rather bohemian.

Ursula explained that her mother had just left for some pastries as she had forgotten dessert but would be home any minute. As if on cue, a key jiggled in the lock and presently Eleanor and two adorable children walked in. Ursula made a show of introducing us: "Anne-Marie, Yves, come. This is Bob." She said it in French, but I noticed how she said it slowly, pronouncing every syllable succinctly to make sure I understood, and so that the children would not be bashful.

"*Enchanté,*" Anne-Marie said, giving me her hand and making a slight curtsy. I noticed she never let go of her doll which she held tightly in her other arm.

"Enchanté," I repeated as I shook her hand. Ursula quickly interjected that Anne-Marie was best known as "Mimi."

"*D'accorde!*" I said, "It will be Mimi from now on. . ."—absurdly too much work to say in French. But with our eyes and smiles, it was well understood.

Yves, the young man, was equally charming. "*Bon jour!*" he said and immediately turned to Ursula to ask if I flew airplanes. I understood his question and began to formulate an answer, but Ursula responded before I could. "*Non.* But he's very good at making sure they land well. He's a control tower operator." To this, his eyes widened, and he exclaimed, "*Ô!* But does he have a car?"

Mimi kept to herself, stroking her doll's hair and keeping her eyes lowered. When I tried to engage her, she looked off to the side. Meanwhile Yves' questions persisted. "Tata, you did not say. Does Bob have a car?"

I heard my name and tried in my best French to answer, "*Je n'ai pas une voiture.*"

"*D'accord,*" he said, suddenly shy.

Ursula graciously asked me to have a seat and waved her arm in an arc to include the full room. "Anywhere is fine."

I took my place on the nearest cushion. It was tucked behind the large square coffee table that looked more like an oversized ottoman. Yves quickly made himself comfortable right beside me. I could tell he still had many questions to ask. Mimi took a seat at the far side, still reserved, and Ursula, in a motherly way, sat next to her. I was worried things could feel uncomfortable and was already dictating stories I could tell to entertain the little ones, when Mimi suddenly poked Ursula in the side. Ursula leaned into her to hear what she was whispering, and then laughed out loud. "Mimi wants to know why your French sounds so funny."

"Well," I said. "That's a very good question."

The children both became engrossed. With Ursula translating, I proceeded to tell a story. "I come from across the ocean where the people speak a different language. There I lived on a farm when I was your age. Do you know what that's like? Cows, a horse, pigs, sheep and chickens. . ."

"Did you milk the cow?" Mimi blurted.

"Oh, yes! I most certainly did! And I talked to her."

"What did you say?"

"I said, 'good morning.' "

"Did you speak to the chickens?"

"The chickens spoke to me! Every morning, one of the hens would say, first thing, 'Squawk! Squawk!' "

Ursula translated, "*Cri! Cri!*" and both the children clapped their hands with glee.

"Do you know what she was saying?" I leaned in.

"*Non!*" Now both the children's eyes went wide and followed my words to the last syllable, unblinking.

"She said, 'I have an egg.' And do you know what I'd do?"

"*Non!* What did you do?" They asked in unison.

"I said, 'Let me see your egg,' and she'd get up and strut off. And guess what? There was always an egg! Always an egg, and so I'd say, 'Thank you, and thank you. And good day!' And I'd go back to the cow."

Suddenly the doorbell rang and in stepped a dark-eyed woman wearing a hijab and holding a basket full of many things, including a baguette that peeked out the top. She was introduced as Zora, the caretaker of pretty much everything in the household, including cooking our lunch.

I stood and said, "*Enchanté.*"

Zora repeated the same, but quickly busied herself with her

shopping bags and rushed off to the kitchen which was through a small swinging door. Within minutes, she returned to the parlor with a *berad*, a Moroccan teapot of mint tea on a silver tray along with five small glasses, which she skillfully filled from a high standing position, not spilling a single drop.

"Evidently she's done this before," I said, to which both Eleanor and Ursula had a good laugh.

"It's such a lovely tradition, isn't it? That every visit is welcomed with a cup of tea and a sweet pastry?" Ursula remarked.

I agreed. It was sweet. Even the room smelled sweet, like orange blossoms.

We sipped our tea. I answered Eleanor's questions about Massachusetts and my family, and before long, Zora announced lunch was served. The table was small, but functional if the kitchen door was left open to allow the fifth stool some room. All the stools that surrounded the table were small and backless. I grabbed the furthest one and took a seat. Yves, of course, wanted the one right next to me.

Zora first brought out an endive salad with a lemon and olive oil dressing. It had been deliciously sweetened with honey and was followed up with a platter of sandwiches on soft Moroccan baguettes filled with French ham (there was no such thing as Moroccan ham. Moroccans don't eat pork), but the cheese was Moroccan, which Zora called *Jben*.

Meanwhile Mimi stayed quiet, so I tried to engage her by asking her doll's name. "It's Claude. It came from Tata's best friend, isn't it so, Tata?"

"Oh my, yes. I had a dear friend when I lived in Paris. Her name is Claude-Elie. We were 'joined at the hip,' " as they say.

"How interesting you know a silly American saying like that!" I said.

"Thanks to my boss. . ." That smile, that smile. . . I just drank it in.

Yves began to pull at my sleeve. He wanted to tell me he

didn't like the ham, or the cheese. That he preferred butter, and he proceeded to remove the soft inner part of both sides of his baguette and smear a hefty dollop of butter on each, laying the lumps around the rim of his plate.

"But, Yves, my dear! You must also eat the salad!" Ursula scolded him.

"*Mais Tata! Je n'aime pas la salad!*" he retorted emphatically. Tata, the name both children called Ursula, was a word that did not have a translation or meaning. I assumed it was something easy for a child to pronounce. I understood the relationship was complicated; Ursula had been separated from them for close to a year. They were half-siblings, I knew, but how that story came to be was a mystery. It was clear the family was close, and that was enough for me.

Tata simply laughed. "Of course! But then, you must not want *les petits fours*. Is that so?"

"*Mai oui!* I want it all," he exclaimed and brought both fists down, doing that thing children do, pout behind giggling lips. The scene was so lighthearted; Ursula and Eleanor were enjoying it, as was I. And no one went without dessert that day.

The party was moving into the parlor, when Eleanor asked if I smoked.

"Absolutely," I said.

"Well then, let's take a moment out on the balcony." Eleanor extracted a blue packet of *Gitanes* from a side pocket of her dress as she made her way through the parlor to the balcony door. The children ran to what appeared to be "their" spots around the ottoman-style table. Mimi pulled out her books that she wanted to show "Claude," and Yves ran his toy car—an exact replica of a Citroën—along the length of the low table. I walked out to the balcony behind Eleanor and pulled a Zippo and a pack of Lucky Strikes from my shirt pocket, launching two cigarettes into my hand. "Try one of mine?"

"I prefer my *Gitanes, merci.*" Eleanor said and offered me

one of hers. Ursula stood by and watched. She did not smoke. I politely took Eleanor's offer, lit it and inhaled deeply. I nearly decided to quit smoking in that moment. My head was spinning; my eyes blurred. As soon as I could speak again, I said what I could without having a coughing fit.

"Ursula, tell me about your job on the base."

"Oh, yes! My boss is the head of the motor pool. I have a fantastic job. Captain White is who I work for. I take care of booking and arranging deliveries, maintenance, returns—cars, trucks, jeeps, buses. Shorthand, you know. . . It's quite busy. I often return home exhausted."

"That's so interesting!" I said, hoping by now I didn't sound like a broken record. "I wonder if I've worked with you in the past. My detachment has jeeps on loan. Perhaps it's been you I've had a phone call or two with?"

Ursula laughed, waving her mother's smoke from her face. "It's rather funny, but you would not have asked for Ursula, if you had."

"Why's that?" I asked.

"The enlisted men and noncommissioned officers at the motor pool don't call me Ursula. Rather by my middle name, Luisa."

"Yes," interjected Eleanor. "I wanted to name her Luisa after her grandmother, but her father, Hans, wanted it to be Ursula. 'A more fitting German name,' he insisted. I relented, of course. Ursula, too, is a beautiful name, in my opinion. But so is Luisa."

I agreed and then asked pointedly, "Which name should I use?"

Luisa pondered a moment. "It's funny. If you'd have called my office and asked for Ursula, they might have hung up on you." Her simple answer, as if wanting nothing but to make things easy—for both her office mates and for me.

"That settles it then. I'll call you Luisa from now on." It was as if the air itself made a deep sigh. The sun peeked out from behind a sinking cloud. "Luisa. A beautiful name!"

She smiled shyly, and I swear her eyes turned bluer.

The afternoon lengthened, then came to an end. I needed to catch the last bus to the airbase, the 5:00, to which Luisa offered, "I'll walk you to the stop."

On the way, we recalled all that we'd done, thanking each other for the delightful way it had unfolded: the children, Yves' silly questions, "*D'accord*," and the tea, Zora. The *Gitanes*. "Whew, boy! Those are some kind of strong!"

Luisa shook her head. "I've no idea why or how someone even starts with those. It must have been the war."

"Of course. The war."

"Bob? I hope my mother didn't overwhelm you with all her questions, putting you on the spot like that?" I could see she was feeling conflicted. Her eyebrows scowled and she clasped her hands as if wishing I'd say exactly what I did.

"But, no! It was charming the way she seemed genuinely interested in me. And how Mimi chimed in with her questions about the cow. No one's ever asked me about my cow."

"Eleanor can be rather forceful when she wants something. I think she wants to know her daughter won't get hurt. I suppose that's a mother's obligation, isn't it?"

"She has every right. . ." I couldn't finish because suddenly the bus pulled up.

"Call me at the base, Monday?" she said.

"I can't wait." I gave her my biggest, warmest smile. We shook hands. I held on long enough to let her know I really couldn't wait. The touch of her hand against mine lingered long after the handshake was over.

A few of the airmen had an 0900 volleyball game going the next morning, and I hopped over to join in, humming a melody I made up on the spot. I had an extra punch in me, returning and setting up balls with an accuracy even I didn't recognize.

"What's gotten into you, pal?" asked one of the guys. "You got a grin stuck on your face like egg yolk."

"That's funny, pal. It's just my look. Okay with that?"

"Okay with that. Sir!"

Sundays were slow at the tower, always. My shift started at 1200 hours, an especially slow time of day. An empty C-47 cargo plane practiced touch-and-go landings, ordinary stuff. These planes were workhorses. The commercial equivalent was the DC-3 with the hatch that lowered from the back, made famous by the "Candy-Bomber" who dropped 46,000 pounds of candy during the Berlin Airlift in the years 1948 and 1949.

The slow hours with little to do allowed my mind to wander with memories of the day before. The sunlight, the children, the things I wished I'd have said. And sometimes the annoying voice telling me I'd made a fool of myself, worried that she, or her mother, did not in the end, approve.

Then a call came over the UHF (ultra high frequency) speakers. It was from the F-86 squadron group commander, saying we were scrambling four F-86s.

Scrambling meant only one thing: An unidentified aircraft was headed our way. The F-86s were America's top-gun fighter jets. They had been deployed in high-speed dogfights during the Korean War and were now our immediate response in emergencies. Best case, it was a mistake. Worst case? We'd blow it to smithereens.

Several communications later, we discovered it was a friendly-nation craft that had flown off course. The panic, or I should say the excitement, pulled me into function mode, though, and for just that moment, I felt normal again; was thinking normally again.

A perfect time to make that phone call I'd been rather nervous to make. The call to Captain White's office to ask for "Luisa."

Our second date was at the USO. Eleanor and the two little ones came along. Luisa, again stunning, wore white: skirt, blouse, shoes, earrings. For the kids, the USO had plenty of things to do: coloring, sing-alongs, games of tag. However, today was a special one for "Bob," and we all sat together on the patio where a duet with a piano and an upright bass played off in a corner. I couldn't get over the fact that the children were so young and yet, still, Luisa's siblings. She talked to them like they were her children, young people who needed guidance, which neither of them asked for.

Both children, now feeling familiar with me, ran about, sticking their tongues out and making fishhooks with their fingers, pulling at their cheeks. When they had settled and sat back at the table, I tried to engage them by exchanging translations. I said, "cat." They said *chat*. I said, "car." They said, *voiture*. I said, "ice cream." They said, *Quoi*?

"Ice cream, ice cream! You know. . . cold, delicious, *chocolat*. . ." I motioned with my hands, like I was eating and ran my tongue around my lips, then rubbed my stomach and pretended to wipe my mouth.

"*A oui! Glace!*" Both exclaimed.

"*Oui, glace!*" And on we went, pretend-eating glace, laughing, Ursula and Eleanor chiming in whenever there was a chance.

The day ended much too soon.

Next time, I thought, Luisa and I need a date alone. After thinking, and probably over-thinking, I chose the rooftop restaurant in the art-deco El Mansour, the fanciest hotel in Casablanca. I wanted candlelight, some quiet time. I reserved a table at the window where we had a view of the entire city.

A tuxedoed waiter with a linen cloth draped over his arm brought us rose-scented water on a silver tray and handed us the menus, printed on deckle-edged parchment. Luisa noticed they offered oysters on the half shell and her eyes sparkled. "Well, order them, then," I encouraged her. "Order a dozen!"

I won't eat raw fish. I don't eat raw anything. But I enjoyed watching my date relish her oysters. We ordered more and more food and then dessert and all the while we talked about everything, our histories, her long stay in Paris, my life on the farm. We watched the sun dip past the end of the sea, and the city light up.

When we finished, I motioned to the waiter for our check. With two gloved hands, he graciously handed me a silver tray with the bill on it. I nearly choked when I saw what it came to, and immediately worried how embarrassed I was about to be when I had to admit I wasn't able to pay.

I squared my shoulders and made a suggestion. I was wearing my gold Bulova watch, a graduation gift from my Ma, that glittered all evening as I reached across to pour Luisa's water and slide the candle slightly closer as we talked. I took it off my wrist and handed it to him.

"You see, Sir," I inhaled. "May I give this to you for now? I haven't the cash on me. But I assure you, I'll get paid on Monday. Would you be so kind as to give me some. . . reprieve?"

It was a stressful moment, to say the least, but the waiter, ever so charmingly, said, *"Mais bien sûr, monsieur."* He pocketed my watch and moved on, probably knowing I now had to explain my situation to my date, who apparently did not miss a beat. "That was the most elegant, honest exchange, Bob. Such a brilliant solution."

"Guess I have my moments," I joked, and then, in all seriousness, reached for her hand and said, "I'm reminded of what Abdul, my main man at the base, told me once. It's a Moroccan proverb: 'Maktub is the creator who writes the script. Nothing is coincidence.'

"Tonight feels like that. Like nothing was a coincidence. I mean, that we met and all, and now we're here. . ." I was starting to get self-conscious, like I was putting the moves on her and coming on way too strong. I really wasn't doing that at all. I was sincere and blabbering all the same, wishing to take back my words.

Luisa smiled her knowing smile, patted my hand and said, "Only you, Bob, could turn this night into a forever memory. Only you could have made a joke out of a tight situation, and yet have it feel so right in the end."

I could swear her eyes twinkled as she said this. I was a happy man.

We started seeing each other regularly. Each weekend, once my duties at the control tower were done, I cleaned up and got ready to see my girl. The USO in downtown Casablanca was our place. The building itself was a classic, white like nearly everything in Casablanca was "*casa blanca.*" Tall palm trees embraced the entrance; inside, an arched doorway led into the garden where lunches, teas, and cocktails were served under a canopy of bougainvillea. Often a two- or three-piece band played in the background. The USO, too, had a large entertainment room with a stage for real stars like Billy Eckstine, the big-band crooner whose smooth baritone voice was what the 1950s was all about.

To the side were cozy areas for activities like movies, dances, and bingo, which were held weekly, and everyone played like it was serious. We won real prizes like toasters, pillow sets and movie tickets. For Mimi and Yves, who often accompanied us, it was always quite special, especially when they were allowed to order their favorite dessert: a rainbow-colored scoop of ice cream—strawberry, vanilla and chocolate—swirled into a silver cup. Stuck on top was a Japanese paper umbrella. Yves cleverly unwrapped the stub of the umbrella each time and was astonished that the thin strips of newspaper he pulled out had Japanese characters on it. Every time he'd ask, "Do you think it will be Japanese again?" It always was.

Ain Diab was a long expanse of untouched beach that ran along the Atlantic coast of Casablanca, another location that immediately became "our" place. Oh, how I loved saying that word, *our*. Here we went to stroll, hold hands, and talk, stroll some more. A hawker may have walked over to ask if we'd like some orange juice, squeezed fresh as we stood by, watching. Of course, we always said yes. We'd thank him, take our juice, which cost all of one dirham (about a penny for both), and continue our stroll. Oh, we had so much to talk about! I told her all about the military and she told me about the London Blitz.

Our special spot was found nearly from the moment we arrived that first day with our picnic blanket and sandwiches: two palm trees that leaned into one another, and, if you looked closely, you'd see their bowing fronds made the shape of a heart. It was under these palms that we sat and dreamed away until the full moon rose from behind us, the sky as pink as the roses I had bought her.

My Humphrey Bogart Moment

DECEMBER, 1954

We dated now as a couple along with other friends who, too, were couples. Jay and Suzie from New Jersey, and Claude and her boyfriend Jimmy from the Air Force. Eleanor, sometimes with a date, sometimes not. The Seaman's Club was our go-to place on these nights. Located on the docks, it was popular with merchant sailors, US Air Force enlistees, French military, and civilian Casablancan nightclubbers. Everyone wanted to be seen at the Seaman's Club, where on any given night, a twelve-piece band with horned instruments, a piano, drums, and a violin played. Big band was all the craze in the 1950s, and anywhere that played and sang our songs of love was sure to draw a crowd.

One evening, sitting with our friends, a song was played that I'd never heard before. It was by Chopin. The band conductor called it, "Tristesse, Étude Op 10, No 3."

"Tristesse" means "sadness," and the song certainly could have said that. But the way they played it, with jazzy instrumental riffs, was uplifting, yet soulful, ending on a self-reflective note. Both Luisa and I loved it from the start, and asked them to play it every time we came. Which we did often.

When the music was over, when the last of our Moroccan coffees had been drunk and the bill paid, we parted ways—Luisa and I turning north where I walked her home and held her close, kissed her goodnight, and walked to the taxi stand with my head in a world of gratitude—for her, for how my life had turned out, for nearly everything I could think of, like that "Morocco" was just another word for "magic."

Casablanca became cool enough in December to wear a sweater. Sometimes it drizzled, but Casablanca always had something enticing going on. Christmas was not high on the festivities list here, but December was a special month for me, reminding me of home and Christmas, and today was the seventeenth, only a week away. How Ma would be all secretive, thinking we didn't know she was hiding stuff in the closets. So, here in Morocco, where the weather was still relatively agreeable, Christmas didn't have the allure it did back in Worcester, but the feeling in my heart was of family, a time to celebrate, twinkly lights, and music.

Luisa and I had a date planned. Although we went to the Seaman's Club often, this night was going to be a holiday sort of evening, a dinner I'd been saving money for. I wanted to splurge. I was dressed in my gabardine suit and had a small rose to give her as thanks for the wonderful few weeks we'd already had together. I shined my shoes that morning until they glistened. I went to the barber to get a "a little off the top," and I arrived at her home a few minutes early, just before our 7:30 date. I was eager as a puppy.

Zora answered the door. I was surprised to see her. Sheepishly she told me, "*Luisa n'est pas ici, Monsieur Bob.*" She wasn't home? I was confused. Very confused. I asked for Eleanor. She, too, was not home. She was on a date with an airman. Probably at the Seaman's Club; she didn't know. The children were in bed.

Stunned, I let her close the door on me.

I didn't know what to do. I started walking. And walking. In the direction of the Seaman's Club. I sure didn't want to go home yet. I'd have a beer and settle my nerves. Then think what to do with myself.

I sat at the bar and listened to the band for a while. Nothing was stirring me, nothing mattered. Even the beer was flat. I thought to look around, see if there was someone to start up a conversation with, and as I spun my stool, I spotted Luisa. Sitting at our favorite table, the one in the corner by the window. And she was with a dapper-looking man, an airman in a Class-A dark blue uniform with a dark tie and light-blue dress shirt. He was handsome, to be sure, with smooth hair. She, as always, looked lovely. *How could she?*

She saw me and returned my gaze with anguish on her face. Or was I imagining it, just to feel better? She was in a green dress with a large green beaded necklace, her hair shone golden. *How could she?*

I made a second attempt to look her way and saw the same expression on her face. I suddenly felt angry. My palms began to sweat. I was going to walk over and demand an explanation. Yes, that's what I was going to do. Right now. Just one more sip. And then, right now.

I spun my stool back to the bar and thought this through. What kind of scene would I leave as my personal legacy? Suppose I had another date one day, wanted to bring her here, what would they remember me by? That time I punched some Romeo in the face? It was not my style.

I finished my beer and left the club. To hell with all of it.

Monday was a blue, blue Monday, no joke. I went to work as I always went to work; I intended to do my best, as I always did, but my heart was bleeding. I did my work with half the enthusiasm and none of the interest. My mind was in a funk. Everything I'd thought was so good, so magical, was now not that at all. It was dismal, gray, wishing to be done with this sad country where I had to work hard to be understood in a language that wasn't mine. I wanted home again with my Ma and Dad. My family. . .

A call came over the intercom. "Romeo Juliet," the voice said, identifying himself as the ops manager in the office below the control tower, Ramon Jaimez, one of our personnel from Spain.

"Go ahead. Over."

"Baker Love [Bob Langway], I have a young sweet lady here who came over with a co-worker from the motor pool. She says she knows you."

"Roger that, Sir."

"She has a letter for you. Sir."

"Thank you. Baker Love. Over."

A "sweet lady from the motor pool" could only be one lady, and a lady I did not want to see. Not now, not just yet. I was still smarting. I wished my shift not to end, just to keep going, keep working, keep busy. But invariably, the clock turned 1700 hours, my time to quit. I proceeded down the stairs, dreading what I was sure to find; a "Dear John" letter. And why would she feel it necessary to do that? To twist the knife even deeper?

But there it was on Ramon's desk in her flowy handwriting: *Bob Langway*. I stuck it inside my vest pocket and hitched a ride to my hut, where I lay down on my bunk. *Do I open it? Do I throw it out? Do I put it away for a later time, when I can handle it better?*

There would not be a time when I could handle it better; that was the truth. And I was a man, needing to man up. So, I ripped it open and set my jaw.

"Dear Bob," she wrote. So far, easy enough. "I'm heartbroken. Will you forgive me? I never meant to harm you. It was a mistake, a very, very bad mistake. I'm so sorry for Saturday night."

She explained that the man (the bastard!) was a pilot she'd dated before we met. He was returning to the States the next day and asked to have dinner one last time.

"We'd made the plans quite some time ago, and I forgot completely about it. He showed up at the apartment at 7:00, while I was waiting for you! What could I do? We don't have a phone; I couldn't call you. I asked Zora to explain, but she messed the whole thing up. She's not used to women dating men, or to men dating women. It's not her culture. She didn't know what to say, or how. Please know I didn't intend to betray you. I'm so sad. I want so badly to see you again. Will you?

"If it's acceptable to you, will you call me when you can?

"With a heavy heart, Luisa."

I jumped off my bunk. I wanted to kiss every airman in the barracks. I wanted to dance, to sing. . . to never go to sleep again. Not until I could tell her, I understand. I forgive you. I love you.

I vowed to call her the very next day as soon as my shift—no, before my shift—began. The best Tuesday, ever. December 21, 1954.

11

Bastille Day

BOB

1955

In 1912, the French General Hubert Lyautey marched into Morocco and claimed the country to be France's protectorate. This did not sit well with the Moroccans, as you can imagine, and from that time forward protests erupted periodically throughout Morocco, primarily in Casablanca. We'd heard about these incidents but never took them all that seriously. I suppose we should have. Moroccans wanted their independence, and even we, as Americans, were seen as foreign occupiers.

The Moroccan history and attitudes were truly unbeknownst to me when I arrived here. I thought they must love us. After all, we won the war, and Morocco was where we fought our very first battle against the Germans. Wasn't that something to be proud of? The answer to that question would be understood soon enough, as this was the Morocco I landed in in 1954, a Morocco tired of France's yoke, a Morocco that wanted its freedom, and a Morocco with growing hostilities.

It was now March, 1955, and I was beginning to feel anxious myself. My military service would end in less than a year, and I would need to return to the USA. My life had changed, though. Luisa and I had been together nearly every day since that prescient dance at the USO. We took our lunches together in the cafeteria. Evenings, after work, we made our way to Ain Diab to our spot under the twin palms, where we sat until long after the sun sank from the sky. But now March was marching on. Soon the summer would come and go, and I knew there would be a day I'd be gone. It left me worried and afraid—afraid I'd never see her again, and this thought was impossible to live with. It was never something we talked about. We acted as if we'd be together always, but fate has its way of moving forward.

It was one evening as we were walking to the Casablanca USO, Eleanor and the children skipping down the sidewalk ahead, that I brought it up to Luisa. "I have a pressing question, my dear. One that has kept me up at night. Lately, it's been every night." Luisa stopped walking and turned to me, knowing it had to be something serious. I never said, "my dear," unless I wanted her attention.

"Would you move to America with me? I mean, to Millbury, to Massachusetts, to the life I once had there, the farm and all. . .?"

With her most alluring smile, she did not hesitate. She came right out with, "Of course!"

"So, you would marry me?"

"Of course, my dear," she giggled. "I would marry you! I want to marry you. I want to spend the rest of my life with you. Yes!"

To say my heart skipped a beat would be too banal a description of how I felt in that moment. That my heart jumped to my throat? Perhaps. That Luisa pranced ahead to tell Eleanor? Absolutely. And me humming to myself "I've Got a Crush on You," a George Gershwin song, sung by such greats as Sarah Vaughan, Ella Fitzgerald, and Frank Sinatra. "How I won you, I shall never, never know. . ."

When I caught up to them, grinning like a fool in love, Eleanor, with motherly practicality, said, "I've been waiting for this for months!" The children, knowing something special had just occurred, clapped their hands and bounced around on their toes, and everyone hugged and kissed on both cheeks, over and over.

The first order of business was the ring, something I had stressed over in a serious way—long before I even asked her to marry me. I wanted it to be perfect, naturally, but I had no idea what "perfect" was to a woman as elegant as Luisa. I thought to beg Eleanor's advice. But the ring was not for Eleanor. I thought about Mike, my buddy at the tower. But he was a jokester. How could I trust something that was to have meaning for the rest of my life to someone like him?

I decided the only one who'd know was Luisa herself, and we made a date of it. After work that Friday, we went to the jewelry counter at the PX and asked to see "the very best, the most beautiful" for the price, of course, that I could pay. I had a little saved up, but $350 a month did not buy a whole lot of diamonds, even in those days.

Leave it to Luisa. Self-composed, she saw the ring she wanted immediately. It was not the first one the salesman pulled out, or even the second or third. It was the one snuggled deep in the back of the velvet box, a thin engagement band with a row of small diamonds that interlocked with the larger wedding band, also with a run of diamonds. The two rings were made of platinum, purer than gold, rarer than gold, more expensive, of course, too, and absolutely stunning on her hand.

We then set our wedding date for July 16. It would be a Saturday and, given it was a few months out, it would give us time to make plans. We spent the weekend writing wedding invitations, addressing the envelopes, chatting it up about the cake and other trivia. It felt so good to giggle over all these nothings. For fun I sent an invitation to each of my family members, all eight siblings, including my Ma and Dad. It was a joke, for sure. No one in my family had ever flown, let alone across the ocean, let alone to Africa. Let alone that it would have been prohibitively expensive, and simply out of the question. But I included a photograph of the two of us, me grinning like a dog wagging two tails. Luisa? Ravishing, of course.

The next order of business was the church. In Catholic tradition, Luisa was to meet with the priest at the cathedral to confirm her faith and ensure a successful marriage.

She and Eleanor arrived mid-morning and were told to have a seat outside the office of the Franciscan priest who had been recommended by Father Cuddy for the interview.

Luisa was invited in and told to sit in a chair facing the desk of this charming, smiling priest. Eleanor, however, was to stay outside in the hallway and wait. Once the door was closed, the priest turned pleasantly toward her and remarked on how attractive she looked. He then sat at his desk, requested her baptismal papers and asked her to give a brief history of her life, including a description of her devotion to her faith.

All the while she spoke, he appeared busy, taking notes and pushing papers. When she had finished, he asked, pointedly, "Are you absolutely sure you want to marry an American? Are you prepared to leave your family and travel to a country so far away? At such a young age?"

Luisa replied that she'd already lived alone in Paris. "I did quite well there," she added.

"Oh?" he responded, as if suddenly awakened. "You were alone there, is it? Did you have male encounters? Perhaps a boyfriend?"

"No. The boys I knew loved the same music. We frequented clubs together, but always just as friends." Luisa thought to add, feeling more than a little uncomfortable at this turn of conversation, "I was always with my best friend, Claude-Elie."

"And what about before Paris? What about England? Did you have male encounters there, those three years on your own?"

"No, none, Father."

"I see," he said.

He then rose from his chair and shuffled his papers as if not knowing where to stop the interrogation, although, clearly, it was over. He came around his desk and stood before Luisa, holding out his hand as if to shake hers. Luisa tried to get up, to shake his hand, too, but his proximity made the whole affair awkward. Suddenly he grabbed her waist, pulled her up to meet his eyes and began touching her body. Luisa let out a cry, pulled him off her and ran out the door, which she slammed behind her, hard.

Eleanor understood immediately what had happened and rushed to console her. Luisa was trembling as Eleanor held her in her arms. "Hush, my dear. It'll be all right." She stroked her hair, her cheek. "What a terrible thing. And with a priest to boot! But how can we say something now? Right now, when we have a wedding to think about, that's right around the corner? The last thing I want is for Father Cuddy to be embarrassed and then for things to go awry, when the wedding is so close. Afterward, I'll take it up with him. Let's not spoil it all. For now." Reluctantly, Luisa agreed. Mostly, she just wanted to leave.

When I came to her apartment later that day to fetch her for an evening at the Seaman's Club, she looked like she'd been crying. She wore no makeup, no shoes. She was sitting on a stool at the dining room table. I knew something was wrong, and, teary-eyed, she told me.

I was fit to be tied. How could someone, anyone—a priest, for the love of Pete!—do this to my girl? I wanted to rush to the rectory and pound on his door. When he answered, I'd tear him out by the collar and twist it till his face turned scarlet. Then I'd ask what he'd had in mind.

But that was not about to happen. With our wedding only weeks away, Eleanor begged me to let it go. "Don't let this incident spoil everything!" I relented, grudgingly. At least, Luisa was now safe. At least with me she was safe, I vowed. Forever, I vowed. She was my girl.

"No dinner then either, I take it?" I knew the answer, and, to be honest, I really wasn't up for going out either. The vision of that jerk's face, all pious with its fake grin, quite had my head in a tizzy.

Luisa said no. She was too upset, and that settled that. We made some tea and ate from the plate of apples and oranges Zora had laid out for us. Talking through the night, Eleanor included, we seemed to settle a score with that priest, at least in our minds. That man was a small man, I concluded. A pipsqueak. Eleanor wanted me to let it go. I did. At least on the outside I did. I smiled and tried to be my pleasant self, but my hatred for that man found no escape from my mind. And my view of that "cathedral" was now tarnished as well. Something I never brought up to Luisa, but Casablanca never did house a bishop's seat. It was really only "just" a church.

I left the apartment late that night—too late to catch a bus—and walked back to the base. All the while, I held visions of that tiny man's face slowly turning blood-red as I wrung his collar tighter and tighter. His eyes popping out, and I would not have even a tinge of remorse.

Two days before our wedding, July 14, was Bastille Day, the day the French celebrate their revolution. In Morocco, it was not such a revered holiday. Government offices and the post office were still open, and we had an appointment at the municipal building to sign our legal papers. Eleanor was to be our witness.

We walked into that beautifully adorned courthouse with its high ceilings of carved yew wood and sculpted plaster. From behind a large ebony desk, the magistrate pushed the marriage documents across and motioned for us to read what it said. There it was in black and white: both our printed names and ". . .you are hereby authorized to join in marriage. . ."

If you could be on cloud nine, could you also get to cloud ten and eleven? Why it took me so long to know this was the woman

I wanted to spend the rest of my life with, I'll never know. But the moment I decided and then the moment when she said yes, were so fluid, so natural, so much the answer to a question I didn't even know I had—where is my happiness? It was here, and with my signature and hers, the matter was sealed.

Floating out the door, dropping her and Eleanor at their apartment, counting the hours left before we'd be together forever, I drove back to the base in a state of unimagined ecstasy. I was about to be married. I could not get over it.

I now had a car, a black 1947 French Ford V-powered coupe, with a small backseat, shiny as onyx, with, at the time, bad brakes. I decided to drive the back way to the base, not only because it was a road less traveled, but because I needed the quiet to collect myself.

About ten minutes outside the city limits, I noticed flashing lights ahead and what looked to be French military soldiers standing at attention. I rolled down my window and saw a barrier pushed partially across the road. An officer with a machine gun motioned me to stop.

I stepped on my spongy brake pedal, and did not come to a stop, much as I tried. Not for some time did I come to a stop, long enough for me to roll past the barrier by several feet. The French soldier who had his 50mm Chauchat machine gun pointed in the air, lowered it quickly and held it to my temple where I could feel the cold barrel pressed against my ear.

This was the real thing! I had no idea what was happening, but I shouted in my strongest authoritarian voice, *"Je suis un soldat américain!"* He lowered his gun but continued to eye me suspiciously. He called over another soldier who, in broken English, asked for my Air Force ID. It was then that I learned, and only in bits and pieces, that sixty people at a coffee shop in Casablanca had been killed in a terrorist bombing.

It had been a national holiday. The streets of Casablanca were full with strolling holiday-makers, the cafés packed. Café

Gonin, often frequented by the French, was crowded that day. People were anticipating the Moroccan street dancing to begin, when a three-wheeled motorcycle rolled up. Two Moroccan boys jumped off and walked away. Minutes later, when a curl of smoke arose from the motorcycle, two European boys ran over to pull a canvas from the back of the bike, causing an enormous explosion to erupt. The café terrace instantly became a bloody scene of dead and writhing bodies.

There had been unrest in Morocco before. An incident in 1947, where hundreds of civilians were massacred in Casablanca, was one of the worst. Now, here I was at the checkpoint, soldiers all around, and couldn't help but wonder, was this another bloodbath about to happen? Why on Earth now, when life was so good; I was about to be married. And Morocco? What happened?

I was eventually waved through, but I was sure shook up. To hell with it all, I kept telling myself. This has nothing to do with me, nothing to do with my soon-to-be wife. We're getting married, come hell or high water.

But the politics of the times took precedence, and our plans did not go as hoped. Because of the incident, Casablanca was now on lock-down. Everything was closed, including the roads. All Nouasseur personnel that Friday morning were restricted to the base. Only the civilian workers from off base were allowed to leave. In the silence of that day, just one day before our planned wedding, I walked to Captain White's office to commiserate with Luisa over our change of fortune.

Luisa was, as always, happy to see me, and I was all too happy to give her a long kiss. "We'll just do it next week," she said, matter-of-factly. "After all, I actually already am Mrs. Langway!" That Saturday was spent in the barracks, and Luisa and I ate spaghetti and meatballs in the cafeteria.

Security lightened up after the weekend, and our ceremony did take place a week later, as Luisa predicted, on Saturday, July 23. It was a small, but typical, wedding at the Sacré-Coeur Cathedral. In total, we had twenty-one guests, including Father Cuddy. Also in attendance were friends with whom we had spent many a date at the Seaman's Club: Jay and Suzy and Claudette and Jimmy. Mike, the jokester from Long Island, was my best man.

Vince and his identical twin worked at the base, doing identical jobs. The two became buddies of mine, and Vince graciously agreed to give away the bride. And oh, how lovely my bride looked! Radiant in white and pearls, and I swear there was a halo over her head.

Then, of course, there was Eleanor who invited Madame Bouvier from the apartment below. Zora graciously made the food, including baking the cake, a French Charlotte with a thick layer of whipped cream topped with slices of fresh sweet orange. Colette, an office friend of Luisa's, was her maid of honor, Mimi the flower girl, and Yves the ring bearer. Yves, who proudly walked the aisle in his young-man suit and tie with the velvet pillow—one that Luisa mysteriously stitched together in some kind of spare time she never told me about—deftly held with two outstretched arms.

We gave our vows. The priest asked for the ring. As Yves opened the velvet flap to reveal this symbol of our eternal love and commitment to one another, the dazzle of the platinum and the diamonds against the indigo velvet was as if Aladdin himself had added an "extra" to our ordinary. It *was* extraordinary, and with great emotion, I took Luisa's hand, placed the band on her finger, and snapped the two rings together. Our union, our bond, was sealed.

The reception lasted into the night, celebrated in Eleanor's small apartment on Rue Voltaire. True to form, Mike gave a hilarious speech, introducing himself with, *"Anyone who knows Luisa well will know what a wonderful and caring person she is. She deserves a good husband. Thank God Bob married her before she found one."*

There were plenty of well-wishes, tears and more laughs than I could ever remember.

We could not really afford a long honeymoon, and in fact, both our offices were short-staffed at the time. A long weekend away, however, was manageable. But where to? We considered many options, all in Morocco. Tangier, with its romantic history, the movie stars who were known to frequent it and only a short ferry-ride across the Straits of Gibraltar to Spain. We thought of Marrakech and its history as the meeting place for trading Berbers over tens of centuries. Then there was Fez, the oldest city in Morocco.

We finally settled on a seaside destination about one hundred miles south of Casablanca. Mazagan was once a Portuguese port where explorers landed enroute to India in the 16th century. The medina with its arched columns, the fortress walls wide enough for donkeys and carts to pass and a towering fortress intimidating enough to make a coward out of you, this city should be in a movie—about medieval times, dragons and such. It was perfect for us.

We stayed at the then-famous Marhaba Hotel, which was directly on the beach. Unusual for 1955, it also had an Olympic-size swimming pool. On its palm-tree-shaded patio were umbrellaed tables and servers wearing slippers and traditional djellaba.

We arrived at the hotel in the afternoon that Sunday, giving us barely enough time to freshen up and make our way to the Michelin-star-rated restaurant on the main floor, where we had dinner reservations for 6:00 p.m. I wore my navy-blue serge wedding suit, white dress shirt and a white tie. I'll admit, I looked the part. My bride was alluring in her ivory summer dress, pearl necklace, white pumps and golden hair, still pinned up from the wedding, the day before.

We walked the hallway hand-in-hand and approached the stairway that led to the restaurant. Even this was in exceptional taste—a curved mahogany railing with wrought iron balusters, the stairs covered with a plush red silk runner. As we descended, I noticed how the guests and waitstaff all appeared to stop, turn and look. Even when I glanced away and looked back again, they still stared. Walking with Luisa, holding her waist, I felt like a movie star with my Ingrid Bergman. A few people began to clap, both men and women. Then everyone started clapping. We were told later that it had been announced, not much earlier, that a newly-wed couple would be dining with them that evening. All through our dinner, people stopped at our table to offer their congratulations and best wishes. Indeed, I felt like a movie star.

The food was the most delicious meal I'd ever eaten (barring, of course, my Ma's cooking). Luisa ordered Canard á l'Orange, and I chose the Chateaubriand. The waiter brought a French Burgundy which I finished off in our room, where we sat later that evening out on our balcony overlooking the sea. Luisa had her mint tea; she did not drink alcohol. The calm sea, the light of the full moon glowing iridescent off the seagulls' wings, the warm breezes, all made for a magical, mystical evening. Here we sat until nearly morning, sharing our lives, our plans for the future, where we might live, what America would be like.

We were only kids, you know—twenty-one years old; Luisa still only twenty. We had a right to dream.

12

Return Home

❦ BOB AND LUISA

1956

Walking the streets of our neighborhood in Casablanca, you'd hardly know our apartment existed. Its doorway was hidden behind overhanging vines the landlord had never bothered to trim. It was just right for us, though, having our first together-home be secretive and tucked away. The doorway to the building was plain; it could have led into a storage closet for all it announced to the world. But, once inside and up the stairs to our little abode, it became our castle, pre-furnished and cloaked in bright fabrics and flooding sunlight.

Immediately upon entering was the living and sleeping area, all in one. The sofa pulled out to a bed at night; a small table was moved close in the mornings for our coffee. A galley kitchenette filled the wall at the far end. Our kitchenware was what we'd won playing bingo: a toaster, the coffee maker, even the melamine plates came from the USO. Through the glass door that opened to a narrow balcony, we looked down upon a courtyard below. Here the landlady's dog sunned himself most afternoons, moving only when his mistress called with a cookie in her hand.

We had been in our home exactly a day, when we decided it was high time to explore our surroundings. We left the apartment early that morning and walked. It was a brilliant day, warm already at 9:00. The street was awash in quietude, nothing but an occasional barking dog. Even the birds seemed still asleep.

Our journey led us in the direction of the medina in old-town Casablanca, where, ultimately, we planned to end up. Luisa loved to shop for things that "would look wonderful" here, or here, or here. I just said yes. It was a pleasure to watch her mind wander, her thoughts take in all the possibilities, her eyes sparkle with joy.

A red neon sign flashed "La Pizzaeria" ahead, and we decided that this early hour of the morning was perfect for pizza. The restaurant interior held a freshness to it. There were a few small Formica-topped tables, large enough to squeeze in a small family tightly, or, as in our case, two people comfortably. Tubular chairs with vinyl seats were sprawled around, and everything was white. Even the tile floor was white.

A waiter came to give us menus and announce the special sauces for the day. He was a sturdy man, rather tall, and spoke French. The menu, too, was in French. He watched me struggle trying to figure out what the heck *câpre* was, long enough to finally say, "So, you're English?" He spoke with a strong accent that I detected was not quite French. "I will speak for you English only."

I laughed. "*Merci*. And where are you from?"

"I am Greek!" he proclaimed, and proceeded to explain he owned the place, that he and his partner, Nikos, used to work on the American base, but now were in business together making "the most and the best delicious pizzas." He stood back proudly, and then asked the same of us.

"From around the corner," I said.

He belly-laughed and said, "Well then. You must know Casablanca well. And Arabic? Can you also speak it?"

"Oh, yes. But only profanity!" I replied, and said the one curse word I'd heard nearly every American airmen use, *kol khara*. Literally, "eat sh*t."

"You are well versed, then," he smiled slyly and kept at it. "*El'an Abook*. May your father be cursed." Mr. Yannis explained,

"This is profanity at its finest. A father, you see, is everything. Without a father? Nothing."

"But of course, *ya hamar*, you donkey!" Funny how some things come to you when you least expect them. Remembering this one additional curse was enough to get a good chuckle going and I was spared the embarrassment of being unable to remember *fromage* to save my life.

Luisa was kind enough to step in and place our simple order—a cheese pizza and two Cokes. "And a Greek salad, too!" she added. "How could we not?"

When Yannis returned with our food, he explained that this was quite the international feast, "with only the best ingredients!" The flour and olive oil were from Greece. The cheese from Italy. The spices and herbs from Spain and Asia. The tomatoes, feta and lettuce came from local farms.

"And the mouths are from Paris. And Millbury." I added.

Pizza and Coke, the breakfast of champions. We let Yannis know he was the start of a great story that was yet to unfold as we were taking the day to explore Casablanca.

"But then there must be a sequel!" he exclaimed.

"Guaranteed to be a sequel!"

Indeed, there would be many. Yannis became our surrogate favorite neighbor at our restaurant du jour, a place we visited at least once a month.

As we left the pizza joint, Luisa hooked her arm into mine, and whispered: "Aren't we so lucky?"

"We are!"

"But I'm worried about something. Like Yannis. One day, we'll not see him again. And there is so much that one day will just go away."

"That's true." I gave her a squeeze. "Where would you like to go first, then? And do?"

"First?" she asked, as if it were an impossible thought and had never once occurred to her. "Well," she said. "I'd love to see my family in London. Why, I've not seen my two little cousins—I'll bet they're not so little anymore—since I was a young teenager! Monica was just a baby then. And it would be so wonderful for you to meet my Aunt Hanni and Uncle Werner!"

I tucked that information under my hat. Somehow, I was going to make that happen. But I didn't want to tell her just yet.

We spent the rest of the day holding hands and swinging our arms as we chattered away about all the things we still wanted to do, with so little time left to do them.

Meanwhile, an idea was brewing in my head. I wanted to take Luisa somewhere special, somewhere we'd never been. Marrakech kept popping to mind. I'd been told that, "as white as Casablanca is, Marrakech is its opposite with colors." I'd heard about the old medina and the city square called Jemaa el Fna, the snake charmers and dancing monkeys, the acrobats, bag sellers, fortune tellers. The food stalls.

I, too, wanted desperately to see it.

FEBRUARY, 1956

We stayed in a riad the long weekend we were in Marrakech. Riads had once been the homes of wealthy merchants and thus were usually located centrally in the medinas of any city. Their entrance was always intentionally unassuming. From the outside, you could easily miss it, but once inside, you'd be met with lavish gardens, fountains and pools, a courtyard with trees, even a chirping bird or two.

From the courtyard and up some steep and unevenly spaced steps, we found an ornately carved door with a padlock and key. This was to be our room. The floors and walls up to the wainscoting were tiled in hand-made zellij tiles. The colorful carpets, the low couches with large cushions, made an enchanting anteroom to our bedroom. A drapery hung over the bed that, when pulled open, revealed a vivid bedspread and pillows. One could imagine the head of the household sitting with his harem, his plates of olives and fruits surrounding him, a flute playing softly in the background.

Once we were settled, we decided to stroll through the medina that we'd heard so much about. We were told by our host not to get lost. She must have been joking because that is precisely what we did. The medina had an endless array of alleyways, leading every which way, with tiny souks, selling everything imaginable: leather goods, tagine pots, carpets, spices, charm bracelets. And even the unimaginable: heaps of pigments—ochre, carmine, cerulean, lapis lazuli—rose oils and argan oil that promised to take the wrinkles off your face, cure indigestion, and even keep your philandering husband at home.

In the square we sat on three-legged stools at a dimly-lit counter. Before us, a man stood at a coal-fired grill, roasting bits of lamb. Steaming plates of couscous and lamb skewers were brought to us along with a cold Casablanca beer for me and an Orangina for Luisa. From a shuttered balcony above wafted Moroccan *chaabi* folk music. Flickering lights and bleating donkeys, shouting merchants and shoving tourists, this was what filled our day. And at its end, it was quite the pleasure to return to our *riad*, a silent sanctuary to a bustling scene that could have been a page out of the Old Testament.

On the following day of this long weekend that felt like another honeymoon, a guide took us to visit a Berber village. Here, stooping houses ran alongside a trickling river that was at the foot of the Atlas Mountains. We were invited into a home that had nothing but a dirt floor with a few wool carpets covering it in strategic places. A wood fire crackled in the corner upon which, I assumed, the meals were prepared. On the wall hung a simple shelf with several metal plates, an assortment of small tea glasses and a large metal spoon. The man of the house, in a polite, soft-voiced manner, proceeded to show us the rugs his wife, sister, and daughter had woven. They were, indeed, beautiful as he displayed one, then another. Whether he wanted us to buy them, we did not know. Neither of us would even consider such an extravagance at this time in our lives, but we thanked him profusely, and left a tip.

Our last night in Marrakech was spent in a restaurant outside the medina, in a traditional residential neighborhood. Immediately upon exiting the taxi a hush befell us. A thought came to me that I'd had a few times now that I'd been in Morocco: It's a country of contradictions. As bustling as the medina was, we were now in a place where silence prevailed. I began to believe that silence was as much a part of the Berber culture as was its secrecy. The Berbers, we learned from our guide, used to write notes in an ink made from a tea that became invisible when it dried. Only when the paper was placed over a flame at the precise distance and correct temperature, would the script reappear. Secretively, silently, our waiter breathed at us, "Come this way. . ."

"Is it morning?" Bob asked in his gravelly morning voice. He whispered it, actually, into my pillow. The glass of our patio door was just beginning to blush. I answered, "Yes," although I was still deep in dreamland.

"I want to give you something. But we need to go to the base for it."

"Now?" I asked. Bob had a way of making surprises real and always wonderful. "After or before coffee?"

"I'll buy you one on the way." He poked my rib. I knew, then, this was a special thing, something he'd been brewing up for a while. I dressed quickly in a pair of slacks and a light sweater, a pair of earrings. We scurried out the door, hustled down the alleyway and climbed into a taxi.

"Nouasseur Air Base, monsieur." Bob was determined, one

of the many things I loved about him. When he had his mind made up, it was made up. No two ways about it.

As we entered the gates, rather than direct the driver to the tower or the USO where we often went, he directed him to drive us to *my* office. What on earth? Did I forget something? And why now, on a Sunday, when the place was virtually empty?

"Where's your best girl?" Captain White asked, smiling broadly as he opened the office door. It threw me for a loop, suddenly wondering if I might be in trouble. Had I missed a call? Mismanaged my duties? But Captain White was grinning like the devil. "Come into my office," was something that only happened when you were about to receive a promotion, or you did something very, very wrong.

He then proceeded to pull out a complicated-looking aeronautical map and laid it flat on his desk. Seeing it upside-down, there was topography, notations on airports, radio navigation aids, and all sorts of other things that I did not have the simplest clue what they were. Captain White never quit with his toothy grin, and while he studied the map intensely as if pretending to find something important, he motioned for us to follow his finger as he traced a route.

He started right where we were: Nouasseur. Up through the Iberian Peninsula, over Germany, and here he pointed out that this spot, "this very spot," he said, as he punched the paper with his index finger, "is where we landed a year ago, Bob. You and all your buddies in tow." He was referring to the time they flew north for Oktoberfest, when Captain White bought himself a Mercedes and drove it "like a bat out of hell" on the Autobahn, a highway with no speed limits. "Could have been Le Mans," I've heard him say more often than once. Automobiles were his passion, second only to airplanes. Then his finger moved further north and stopped at Frankfurt. "And here is where I'm dropping you off."

"What?" I felt the blood leave my face. I looked at Bob. He, too, was grinning. "What are you saying?"

"We're about to take a private flight, my dear, piloted by our private captain, to. . ." And here he hesitated, like he didn't want to break the spell, but I couldn't wait any longer.

"Bob, you must say!"

"I'm taking you to London."

"London. London?!" I must have repeated that word enough to make up an entire paragraph. I could not believe it, or him or Captain White. How? What? "We're going to London? But when?"

"My love. You've wanted to see your family. We absolutely must see your family. They, who were there for you when your Mummy was away, there for you when the bombs fell, your cousins, the two 'little ones,' as you say. Yes, my dear. We're going to London! And we're going soon. Captain White has a C-47 arranged for us, a plane we will have all to ourselves. We'll go home; we'll pack; we're leaving on Tuesday. Oh! And I asked your boss. You've got the time off," Bob winked.

It wasn't so much the excitement of finally going back to see the family I'd missed for so long. Nor was it that I'd see London again, the city I only remember in ruins, the many, many days and nights running to the stairwell, to the Underground, the smell of burning things, the smoke, the terror, the not-know-ing-anything. I remembered Mummy saying that "good always wins out," and how right she was. But, at the time? At the time, really no one knew. It was a high-stakes game and for all we knew, Hitler could have won. He could have. The battles were risky. So many men—and civilians, for that matter—lost their lives. So many cities now lay in rubble. And for what? For the sake of fascism, a word that had become household by now.

But this is what caught me and stayed with me—that Bob would go to such an extent to make me happy. He was my man, indeed. He could recite the dictionary to me, and I would sit and drink it in.

The C-47 was Captain White's plane. He told me so often I had it memorized, that it alone won the Second World War for us. It transported troops and cargo, dropped paratroopers, towed gliders, and evacuated wounded patients during both the Second World War and the Korean War. He bragged about how it could fly on one engine, withstand mid-air collisions, and land on its belly.

It was Valentine's Day, the day Bob, Captain White, and I walked out on the tarmac and climbed the long stairway of the gangplank that lowered from the rear. Given the plane was essentially empty, we had our choice of seats. We nudged each other, "Here? . . . Or here?" I was ready to flop my overcoat down just anywhere, in any seat, but Captain White would have none of that.

"What? You're about to leave me, all lonesome up in the cockpit? Na-na. C'mon up here, Luisa. You have the co-pilot's seat. Bob? You get the jump seat. . ." We happily buckled in.

"Clear for take off," the signal came from the tower, the signal Bob surely would have given had he been at the controls that day. Up, up we went, the shimmering tarmac below like a mirage, and then the full view of the sky. Far below was the land we had just walked upon. This is what I saw through the 180 degrees of windshield. How quickly the city disappeared, then the ocean appeared with its tiny whitecaps. Within twenty minutes we were 13,000 feet up in the air and about to fly over Spain.

Captain White then did something unexpected. He looked over to me and said, "Here. Take over, will you?"

I gave Bob a quick glance. He didn't look enthused, but this was my boss. How could I say no? I moved into the pilot's seat, buckled the seat belt, with Captain White's instructions: tight, comfortable, and low on the hip bone. "Now grab the wheel with both hands. . . there now. You got it. Set your sights on the horizon."

"Aye, aye, Sir." I faked a salute and stared straight ahead, a bit nervous, if I were to give it any thought.

"What do you see?" Captain White said.

"Nothing, sir."

"See that line down there?"

"No, sir. I don't see a line."

"Look harder."

"I don't see a line, Sir."

"There. The border between Portugal and Spain. Can you see it now?" I looked and looked again hard, actually expecting a real line, black and vivid. But all I could see was what looked like a valley and a mountain range, brown and rugged. I realized, then, he was joking.

"No, Luisa. No lines. That's what always gets me. We fight and argue and tell all kinds of stories about how important these borders are and who can cross them and who can't. But when you see what I see from up here, God's Earth is nothing but one enormous ball of magnificence, pulsating with life that goes on and on and on and on, deep into the ocean and the forests and cities, and high into the skies. Then, what comes along are all our own rules and stories to muck it all up."

Captain White relaxed then, sat back in the co-pilot's seat and encouraged me to "steer on," while he basked in the delivery of his latest sermon, as he was known to do. As for me? I basked in the sensation that here I was, maneuvering this plane that was soaring over all that majestic land below, and, in the moment, I felt like I could do anything. The world was in my hands. Claude-Elie's face came to mind and her innocent remark, "I'd love to fly." And my thoughts, then, that I, too, could do that. And here I was. My soul, my heart, my life was free, let loose like a bird. And I was with the most wonderful man in the whole world. How did this happen? What he said to me, what we said to each other, about how lucky we were, to be alive now. Nothing in the world was more perfect than this.

My fifteen minutes of glory came to an end. Captain White, having broken every Air Force cockpit regulation ever written by allowing me to pilot a 20,000-pound military cargo plane, asked to have his seat back, as if all he did was make a quick run for the restroom. We landed at Bordeaux, refueled, flew to Rhein-Main Air Force Base, landed, hugged him goodbye, and Bob and I walked off to catch Pan Am to London.

Waiting for us at Heathrow was my British family—all of them. Aunt Hanni now had a few white threads in her still thick, dark hair. Uncle Werner looked much the same, only softer in the middle. My cousins? They weren't babies anymore. Hazel was slender and tall, a young woman already at sixteen. Her hair, a lovely chestnut color, long and braided down her back. Monica was a little bug, age five now, as rambunctious as she was precocious. Her voice, chirping constantly, "But Mummy! But Mummy!" when she wanted something, anything. To feed the pigeons, a push on a swing, a chance to hold her big cousin's hand, although she insisted on calling me "Auntie."

Our plan was to visit for ten days. These were days during which we'd meet, for the first time, relatives like Uncle Werner's brother, who once sailed to the Spanish island of Majorca and chose to stay. Werner also had a cousin whose acting career took off after she left Berlin. Her real name was Lilly Peiser, but later she took her stage name of Lilli Palmer, the name the world knew her by. She was married to Rex Harrison, and acted in many Hollywood films, winning a Golden Globe Award for her role in *But Not for Me*. All this was family, a family rifted apart by history. How good it felt to weave the frays back together again.

Nothing takes place in England without tea, and upon our

arrival that first day, that's exactly how it began: a pot, wrapped in its cozy, filled with brewing loose-leaf tea, some shortbreads and a fruit pâté. For Aunt Hanni, it was no question that issues of the war, the terrible bombings, the shattered lives, needed to be addressed above all.

Was it crazy, I thought to myself as she talked about so many things that happened, right here in London. Was it crazy to be as grateful as I was in a world that had bombs that could destroy entire cities, and death camps, and despots? There were still murders, starvation, unrest, of course—look what took place in our own country, Morocco. But it all seemed like someone else's life, not mine, and I tried to explain that to her.

"It was as though I was scooped up right in the middle of it all, sent to school, supervised by nuns, and then plunked back down just after, into a city, Paris, that acted as though no war had ever happened."

"You were blessed," she said. And changed the subject. How was our room?

Our room? It was spacious with two wardrobes in it, one being occupied with everything imaginable, including cricket bats and several pairs of wellies. The other had our bedding, soft with large pillows that reached nearly to the middle of our backs. But the bathroom; it was terrible! The water from the handheld shower only dribbled out, and then it was never hotter than lukewarm. The pull-chain for the toilet kept coming off the hook. And oh, was it cold in there, trying to dress on that icy tile floor. I didn't complain, and Bob didn't complain, but the Brits certainly have a knack for discomfort. "Just a ruddy nuisance," I could imagine them saying.

The exterior, on the other hand, impressed us. It was a neat, Tudor-style brick home with a typical "English garden" out front—rows of lavender, roses, and hollyhocks that were close to budding into springtime's freedom. Too bad, I thought, we wouldn't stay long enough to enjoy it.

It was on our third or fourth day that Aunt Hanni wanted to show me around the neighborhoods that had been hit hardest during the war, the buildings that were still semi in ruin, Holborn and Stepney. There were still homes that had nothing but ribbons of curtains fluttering through shattered windows.

Aunt Hanni mused as we gazed around. "Here we are; the war over by over a decade, and still, we see this. We live like the war never happened. Like it's all good again, and things have changed. But things don't really change. You just keep on going, doing your life as you've always done."

"It's a sad statement about us, isn't it?" I said.

"It is a sad statement, Luisa." Aunt Hanni fidgeted with her purse strap and then looked off into the hazy sky. "You know. . . there were good things that happened during that time too. I saw it with my own eyes—wartime can be a time of extreme kindness. People I've seen who came from Germany, Russia, Poland, their stories—my God! I've heard horrible things, things I couldn't believe an ordinary person, someone standing before me, with eyeglasses on, holding an umbrella, could be saying. . . But they've told of marvelous things, too. The courage, the unshakable goodness some people have in them as well. A child taken in; a blanket, a warm home. It really calls attention to humanity at its rawest."

"It makes me wish that wars could be fought by those people who want to fight them. And they could go off somewhere and just do it, all on their own. Leave the rest of us to live our lives," I said.

"Oh, Luisa! You've always had a charmed way of looking at things."

On our last night, Aunt Hanni wanted our send-off to be special. She decided on Veeraswami, the oldest, and, according to her, most authentic, Indian restaurant in London.

After climbing a narrow flight of stairs from the street level of Regent Street, a district rife with expensive boutiques and jewelry stores, we walked into a world of exotic colors and pungent aromas, not unlike Morocco, only, it seemed, more lavish and glitzy.

The maître d' led us into the Paisley Room and sat us at a low table with plush cushions. Bob was directed to sit at the head of the table. I was at his right-hand side, and sitting to Bob's left was Hazel who could not get enough of the fact that he was American and spoke English with such a funny accent. Monica sat to my right, Aunt Hanni across from her, and Uncle Werner at the tail. Aunt Hanni, with her presumed duty to honor tradition, had orchestrated all this. It was cozy with our cushions, the lighting, and most of all, the ambiance—charming and mood-inspiring.

Aunt Hanni relaxed into the comfort of family and started with, "Luisa. It's lovely how you've taken your grandmother's name. To be honest, I never liked 'Ursula.' It never suited you. You were always more sophisticated than that. 'Ursula' sounds like the name of a doll. Or a cat. Luisa? Why, it could be the name of a film star! Or. . . a Maharani!" she said, waving her arm, indicating our royal surroundings, and giggled.

"Oh, Auntie, you certainly have a way with compliments. Yes, I began using her name when no one at the base could pronounce 'Ursula' correctly. It always came out as 'Erssla.' I hated that. Luisa rolls off the tongue much easier, no useless vowels to grapple with."

"Ah, yes, Luisa. . ." Uncle Werner added. "So good to have you here with us. Alive and happy. What terrible times we went through. . ."

As happens so often in European settings, the talk once again came around to the time of war. Everyone, it was assumed, fared rather poorly; everyone had a story, but tonight it was more about us, our own family, now that it was done.

"Do you know how lucky you are?" Aunt Hanni said, musing gently, as if about to say something she'd been thinking about for a while.

"Yes. Of course, I do!" I had miraculously landed a life more amazing than any fairytale, falling into the arms of the man I loved more than anyone in the world.

But Aunt Hanni meant something else. I could see it in how her eyes darted back and forth. She slowly picked at a hangnail and then said, "Luisa. I've never known how or even if I'd tell you about this. Your Mummy was always so protective, you know. And I could just have let it go, by all means, and said nothing. Many people do. But I think I would regret this for the rest of my life if I did not open my mouth, so help me God. It's about getting out of Berlin when you did."

I had no idea what she was about to say. Aunt Hanni looked so sad. I could handle anything, I always told myself. I had lived through the bombings of London. I practically raised myself, alone in Paris. . . "I do remember, Aunt Hanni," I said. "It was rather sudden that Papa got his new job. We practically flew out of there like a flock of swallows."

"Yes. Then you remember Milan?"

"Of course I remember Milan!"

"That your home was but an apartment, do you remember that?"

I laughed. "Yes, of course I remember. It was small, like a hotel room. It's how I thought of it, just a dropping off place before we moved to the house we were meant to have, the playroom and gardens and bike races and beach days we were supposed to have."

"That house never came about, did it?"

"No, no. It never did. My Papa had to leave suddenly. We saw him off at the train, Mummy and me. I was so young then. I did not understand that divorce was something permanent. I always wondered about why he never came back. Everything was about the war. That was the answer I always got whenever I asked about anything. It was always a mystery, the way things evolved. I didn't really understand much."

It wasn't easy talking about my Papa. I had an empty space in my heart where he lived, or, better said, where his memory lived. I'd resigned myself to the fact I'd never see him again. It was just a fact of my life.

"But he was sent away, you know?" Aunt Hanni kept at me.

"Are you trying to tell me he left for another woman? I don't want to hear. . ."

"No, no, Luisa. It was not another woman. It was the government. The Nazis."

Something told me this conversation was about more than my Papa. I looked around the table and saw all eyes on me. Bob reached for my hand underneath the table and held it tight. He, too, sensed something was brewing. Hearing the word "Nazi" and in the context of my father, felt evil, and a creeping fear rose in my chest.

"My dear Luisa, your Papa was obeying the law."

"A law?"

"The law in Germany at the time, that required German citizens who were married to Jews to divorce them."

"That's why they divorced?"

"Yes."

"Was my Mummy Jewish?"

"Yes, Luisa. Eleanor is Jewish. So am I. I am Jewish. Uncle Werner's Jewish. So is Aunt Gerda."

"So. . . I'm Jewish?"

A hush fell over the table that spread like a cloud over the entire restaurant. Dishes stopped clattering; waiters stopped moving. I felt as though my own blood stopped rushing—my Jewish blood. "But we were Catholic!" I thumped the table. "I was baptized. The nuns. . . the convent. Our wedding!" I turned to Bob. Surely, he had something to say. But he looked stricken. I stared into the table so hard I thought a crack could start its way down the length for the power I gave it.

And yet, it made sense suddenly. Grandpa Sally. His last name was Israel, for God's sake, and I never put the pieces together. The stories of Aunt Gerda and Uncle Harry, how they vanished and ended up in Shanghai. The Night of Broken Glass, so famous in history, yet I was too young to understand that it had to do with me too. That all along, I was Jewish. How Sister Eustace should be ashamed for stealing a doll from a Jewish child. I began to laugh at this thought.

My emotions were so high, I didn't know if I wanted to cheer or cry. My laughter continued uncontrollably and nervously, and then I couldn't stop. It was contagious. Everyone began to laugh. As soon as someone tried to stop, they'd start right up again. Even Hazel—I'm sure she had no idea what this was about—giggled hysterically behind her hands. We laughed so hard someone started to hiccup. We all had tears in our eyes.

My God, I am Jewish!

The next morning, I was giddy as we hustled to the airport. It was a rebirth for me. The puzzle piece that had been missing from that empty place inside me had finally fallen into place.

I cannot say I forgive the man who was my father. Why he never tried to contact me again—this I could not forgive. But that he did what he did? I can understand it now. Germany was a different place then. People were threatened with death if they didn't obey the new laws and, surely, we saw what happened with the *Sippenverfolgung*, when Hitler had over 4,900 people killed by firing squad or the gallows, simply for being related to anyone who had conspired in the attempt on his life—wives, children, parents, siblings, cousins, even mere "friends." And what about the young boys, the Hitler Youth in Berlin, who were stood against a wall and shot for not fighting the enemy hard enough?

No. Papa saved his life. I hope he found his happiness.

Everything went so fast that morning. Bags were packed. Good-byes were said, and rush-rush to catch our flight back to Rhein-Main Air Force Base. But I could not stop thinking about the revelation of the night before. "Bob," I said, when we were finally alone. "What did you make of all that?"

"I don't know why Eleanor would keep it from you so long. The war is long over, and Germany is on the mend. Jews are being welcomed back. I can only surmise that she was worried about me."

"You? Why you?"

"You know, dear, what America is like. I've told you. You've seen it. Prejudice, in my country—our country now—is a way of life. I think—and pardon me if I'm overstepping my bounds by making assumptions about your mother—but I think she was worried I'd stop loving you." Bob's chin began to quiver. "I will never stop loving you. I love you all the more now for what I've learned. You're my girl. . ." We fell into each other, weeping, for joy, for loss, for the life we were given. For our histories, and our future.

Bob and I had exactly one month to prepare for our move to America. There was not much to pack. We did not own much; our furniture belonged to the apartment. Clothes? We had very few. The biggest part was embracing yet another new country. True, I spoke the language. But how would I reconcile a country where all I knew was what I saw in the movies: Hollywood. New York. Hot rods and teenagers. And the food? Hamburgers? Not a chance. That would be something I'd never get used to. But I had Bob. And that was everything to me.

I was in the window seat, Bob next to me. As the plane rose in the air, Bob leaned over me and pointed. "Luisa, look," he said.

I did look. I looked to him, then out the window and together we watched as the plane swooped to the right and then up along the coast of Casablanca. We were leaving Morocco just as Morocco was gaining its freedom. March 2, 1956 was its birthdate. April 13, 1956 was ours. And there it was, the sparkling sea, the white sand beaches where we had fallen in love, the toy palm trees, and white stucco buildings. I imagined the donkey carts with their herbs and souks with their sellers, their embroidered *djellabas*, their pillbox hats, the noise, the coffees, our pizza shop. All was gone and we were on to our new life. Morocco had become Morocco again, free from "protectors," and I was to become American.

"We'll always have Casablanca," Bob said, squeezing a tear from his eye.

"Yes. We'll always have Casablanca."

Epilogue

On September 25, 2022, Luisa took her last breath. I was holding her hand, just like we'd been doing for over sixty years. It was the saddest day of my life. For all the joy she gave me throughout our lives together, I will forever be grateful.

We made our home in Massachusetts after we returned to the States. Here I received my bachelor's degree in electrical engineering at UMass, Amherst, and later I earned an MBA from Northeastern University in Boston. Luisa cared for our home and our four daughters and one son. Upon her passing, there were eleven grandchildren. Our first great-grandchild, Kennedy Yorke Williams, was six weeks old when Luisa held him for the first—and last—time.

That we came from such vastly different backgrounds, and that we should meet in such an unexpected and exotic location, a fairytale neither of us could have dreamed up, felt like it was a story that needed telling.

Luisa was a cultured woman for whom fate had delivered a difficult childhood. Rather than succumb to it, she learned at an early age to see the gifts that life provided, even when she was in the direst of dire straits.

I? I was a poor farm boy, raised during the Depression,

with little chance for opportunity. And then the idea to join the military presented itself. My time in the Air Force showed me parts of America I'd never seen and probably never would, and then it showed me countries and cultures I'd never known about: Northern Africa, England, and Germany. Something I learned early on, as a child on the farm, is that "Apple blossoms become fruit." The military taught me in no uncertain terms that that was indeed true: "The other side of hard work is success."

Shortly after Luisa and I arrived in the United States in 1956, Eleanor and her two children followed, taking up residence in Massachusetts for a while before joining her sister in Duluth, Minnesota. She worked the rest of her career years as a corporate, bilingual executive, and died in a nursing home in Massachusetts in 1997.

Mimi married a US Army enlistee and moved to Germany with him, where she worked as a tour guide for Americans on holiday. They had three children, then divorced. Mimi remarried after returning to the United States.

Yves, as a teenager, became enamored with the hippy movement of the late 1960s and early 1970s. He was in attendance at the famed Chicago Democratic Convention (DNC) of 1968, where he rubbed shoulders with the likes of the Black Panthers and the SDS (Students for a Democratic Society). Yves also became enamored with the drugs of the time.

In May of 1969, I received a phone call from Eleanor. It had to do with Yves. We were living in Natick, Massachusetts, and Eleanor lived fifteen minutes away, in Framingham. The night she called she could hardly speak for crying. "He's awfully sick, Bob. I need you. . . The police will be here soon." I had no idea what I was in for, but her plea sounded desperate. Without finishing my dinner, I jumped in my car and drove straight over. By the time I arrived, Yves was in cardiac arrest. He had overdosed on heroin.

Jacque returned to France, where he reconnected with his daughter, Monique, who was born two years before he met Eleanor, a daughter he'd been estranged from throughout the war and throughout his marriage to Eleanor. He later became an Orthodox priest and lived until 2007.

In 1987, the German government invited Eleanor and Luisa back to Germany as a part of its reparation program, called *Wiedergutmachung*, or "making good again." Although Eleanor wanted nothing to do with the past and nothing to do with its "Jewish situation," she took them up on their offer, and she, Luisa, and I flew to Berlin for a two-week visit. There, Eleanor was able to find her first husband, Hans, and arranged a meeting at the famed "Café Kranzler" on the beautiful boulevard, Unter den Linden. After nearly fifty years of silence, Luisa saw her father again. It was a warm reunion—although I had to ask myself why it took fifty years of silence to get here. Afterward, Hans invited us to his apartment in Berlin for *Abendtisch*, the "evening table," which we readily accepted. Eleanor did all the negotiating.

Their apartment building was one of the few that had not been damaged in the war. The walls had grayed and cracked. The arched doorway still had the original brown wooden door with carved figurines and a stained-glass transom. How this particular building survived when the rest of the neighborhood had been decimated can only be called a miracle.

Their apartment was simple with traditional German hominess: flocked wallpaper, worn Persian rugs and a lace runner down the middle of the coffee table (which also served as our "evening table"). Framed sepia-toned photos of old German cities lined the walls. Hans's wife brought out a platter with cold-cuts and cheeses and a basket of dark *Bauernbrot*, "farmer's bread." Hans spoke some English and between that and a lot of hand motions, he managed to communicate that he'd worked for the same firm for forty years. He was about to take his pension.

It wasn't until well into the evening that we learned Hans had a son, Peter, who was twenty-eight years old. He came to the parlor to introduce himself, and then went back into his room, wanting nothing more to do with us. I found it to be so with many of the young people whose families had lived through the war. More often than not, they just didn't want to know. Luisa certainly could have triggered something of the sort in him; a sister from "during that time."

For Luisa, these meetings gave closure. She was all too happy to reunite with her father, but she was also happy for him that he'd found his life. And she hers.

Hans died in 1989.

For all of her life, Claude-Elie remained Luisa's closest friend. Although they never saw each other again, they stayed in contact by writing letters. Claude-Elie reported often how badly she was treated by Mme Caillou and her father, who was well-known in Paris for the art gallery he owned. In time, her letters became less and less frequent, until they stopped altogether. My brother Chet once made the effort to visit her when he was in Paris on business. He took her out for lunch. He later reported that she "acted strange and unfocused. . ." The last we heard of her was that she had been institutionalized. Perhaps the unfocused and strange behavior had to do with the drugs they were giving her. It's at least what Luisa hoped was the case with the dearest friend she had in the world.

It bears mentioning the two matrons of our families: my Aunt Eva and Luisa's grandmother Martha. Aunt Eva, the one who so movingly told me I had Indian blood in me, lived to be one hundred years old, dying in Oxford, Massachusetts in 2000. She had three children. The middle child, Curtis, enlisted in the army when he was eighteen and was sent immediately to the front in Europe. A wound Eva was never able to heal was his death on the battlefields in the Battle of the Bulge, the last Allied campaign against the Germans on the Western Front.

Grandmother Martha went blind after her husband died in 1938. After Kristallnacht, she left Berlin and moved to London with her daughter Hanni, and her son-in-law Werner. Her entire life in England was spent in darkness. What Luisa had to say about that, that her blindness had do with "not wanting to see any more," could well have been true. To witness what happened to the greatest department store in all of Germany, her store, to have suddenly lost her husband, then to learn what the Nazis were doing to the Jews in her own country, could well have been too much for her.

She died peacefully at their home in London, Hanni and Werner by her side.

Did we ever return to Morocco? We did. It was our fiftieth anniversary, the summer of 2007. Mimi had flown to France for her father Jacque's funeral, and we decided she should meet us in Casablanca afterward. We could revisit all our old haunts together, the school, the apartment where she lived when she was young.

We were more than a little disappointed. Everything had changed. The street names had changed; they were no longer French. We wanted more than anything to walk through our beloved cathedral, the "Cathédrale du Sacré-Coeur," where we married. First, we had difficulty finding it. The street had been renamed Boulevard Rachidi. Second, we were met at the door by two armed soldiers who gruffly let us know it was no longer a church. Rather, now it was a Moroccan Cultural Center. And it was closed. At least to us, it was closed.

With Mimi and her second husband, we spent two weeks in Morocco, but it was never quite what we remembered. The magic that we both held in our memories—that would have to stay with us.

Adolf Hitler was found dead alongside his companion Eva Braun on April 30, 1945. The cause of death was a gunshot to the head; Eva Braun's death was caused by ingestion of cyanide. Seven days later, Germany signed an unconditional surrender to the Allies, and all fighting in Europe ceased at 11:00 p.m. Central European Time, on May 8, 1945.

Although the war in Europe was officially over, the war in the Pacific continued for another number of months. In July of 1945, an American air raid over Shanghai killed and injured a large number of the population, including many of the Jewish refugees. It would be the last they saw of the Allied attacks, however, as the atomic bombs were dropped on Hiroshima and Nagasaki a month later, bringing Japan to an unconditional surrender to the Allies on August 14, 1945.

As China had been occupied by the Japanese for the duration of the war, the general population had remained ignorant to the happenings in Europe during that time. When the news that Jews had been murdered in the streets and sent to gas chambers by the hundreds of thousands came to Shanghai, it was met with stunned disbelief. For some of the Jewish refugees, the idea that these atrocities were committed in their own country, Germany, a country that had laws against murder, an educated and modern country, was simply unfathomable.

The news of Japan's surrender, on the other hand, was met with great jubilation. The oppressive occupation was finally over. Yet, following right behind, was a fearful sense of uncertainty. With the retreat of the Japanese, the Chinese Nationalist government quickly collapsed, and a radical new Communist government took its place. It was led by Mao Zedong. This new regime, it became clear, had no place for refugees, and all foreign nationals were ordered to leave.

Mass migration took place, starting in September of 1945, and continued over the next several years. Most of the Jews left for Israel and the United States—mostly by boat. By 1950, there were no refugees left in Shanghai, and all foreign-owned properties and businesses had been confiscated by the Communists.

Gerda, Erich, and Gerda's daughter, Steffi, left the harbor of Shanghai during this time and immigrated to the United States, most likely with the help of UJA, the United Jewish Appeal. Their destination, Duluth, Minnesota, could have had something to do with humor on Erich's part. He was a funny man. Perhaps he figured, if they were to arrive in America, let it at least be as far inland as possible. "That way we'll know we've arrived." After eight-and-a-half days on the St. Lawrence Seaway, they landed in the last city of the trip, Duluth, on the western-most tip of Lake Superior where they made their lifelong home.

Gerda's first husband, Harry, returned to Berlin after his life in Shanghai and became a very rich man, something he always said he wanted.

www.ingramcontent.com/pod-product-compliance
Lightning Source LLC
Chambersburg PA
CBHW051615120626
46551CB00014B/1809